Voodoo

A Guide to the New Orleans Voodoo Customs, Equipment, and Rituals as well as the Numerous Cultural Influences that Shaped it Originally

© Copyright 2023 by Marie Duvalier

Legal & Disclaimer

CONTENTS

INTRODUCTION

Many people will tell you that there is no such thing as New Orleans Voodoo. According to them, the whole thing started as a marketing campaign to woo tourists. Later, a few bored white folks created a "tradition" by reading some books on African and Afro-Caribbean spirituality, then combining that information with African American folk magic, Wicca, hermeticism, and just about anything else they could find that was suitably "mysterious" and "spooky." Those criticisms aren't entirely without merit. And yet they miss the greater point: New Orleans Voodoo has become for many a powerful and meaningful religious tradition.

The critics may have a point. There may not have been a survival of Haitian Vodou that persists to the present day in the Louisiana backwoods and bayous. But, like most creation myths, the stories point to a deeper truth. There is something magical in the Crescent City, some force that powers New Orleans Voodoo and that draws people to its holy land for pilgrimages and parties (which have often been closely linked, despite what you may have heard in Sunday school). The explanations may not be literally true, but that's not important. What's important is that the creation myths point to something that must be explained.

The French philosopher Jean Baudrillard has spoken of simulacra—signs, symbols, and simulations that are treated as and become reality. As he puts it, "Simulation . . . is the generation by models of a real without origin or reality: a hyperreal. The territory no longer precedes the map, nor does it survive it. It is nevertheless the map that precedes the territory—precession of simulacra—that engenders the territory."

Perhaps the legends created New Orleans Voodoo. If so, that creation has long since taken on a life of its own. The myth has sired many children and has called others to listen and to learn beneath the city's wrought-iron balconies. But many believe something else is behind the stories. They have felt the reality behind the magic; they have drunk from the water of Lake Pontchartrain, and now the city has claimed them for her own.

You may feel her calling out to you in your dreams. You may long for her brightly colored shotgun cottages and the jazz bands playing in her streets. Or you may just be looking for a new spiritual diversion. Your motivations are your own; whatever you want, you'll find that New Orleans is happy to oblige you. But be careful. Those who know the city will tell you that there's plenty of danger to go with the beauty. If you don't watch yourself, you may just wind up sucked into something you never bargained for. She's a sweet mistress, but she can be a harsh one too. Take her joyfully, take her lovingly, but don't you dare take her lightly.

Because, you see, that's the way real magic is. Real magic is as joyful and sad as a jazz funeral, as pretty and as dangerous as white oleander. If you want to experience the spirit world, be ready for beauty that will bring tears to your eyes and for terrors that will scare you witless. There's plenty of both in New Orleans, and those who will share in her dreams had best be prepared to face her nightmares too. Lots of visitors who overindulged in Bourbon Street's bars have awakened without their wallets and cell phones, and many spiritual tourists who took New Orleans Voodoo for a harmless game found themselves face to face with things they hadn't expected. Those who escaped alive rarely got out unscathed. Like many who came before them, they left with scars as souvenirs of their journey to the Big Easy.

Unlike Haitian Vodou or other more organized Afro-Caribbean traditions, New Orleans Voodoo is a freeform system of worship.

You can incorporate whatever works for you into your personal practices, and nobody will tell you that you're doing it wrong. On the other hand, no one is going to tell you that you're doing it right. Like any conjure person, you'll have to judge that by how your magic does or does not work. New Orleans Voodoo is not about adherence to a doctrine or a script; it's about working with the spirits to bring about changes on the material plane.

For those coming to New Orleans Voodoo from a more structured tradition, this can be simultaneously exhilarating and terrifying. You can declare yourself a conjure man, a root doctor, or a Voodoo Queen—but then you'll be expected to deliver the services appropriate to your self-proclaimed title. You'll be judged not by who initiated you or how well you have memorized the proper prayers, but by whether you can do the work for your clients and yourself. If you can't, you're just an empty title, a poor deluded soul pretending to have power you'll never have.

I have provided you with introductions to some of the spirits most commonly honored in New Orleans Voodoo, as well as safeguards that may help you to avoid psychic or physical injury. But, in the end, the instructions I've provided here are merely guidelines. It's up to you to make the acquaintance of the spirits, and it's up to you to accept responsibility for the changes they may bring into your life—and you can rest assured they will bring changes. When you call on the lwas, don't be surprised when they answer.

TRADITIONS: MARDI GRAS

The pre-Lenten celebrations that end with Ash Wednesday are found in many places around the world, but as so often happens, New Orleans has put a special spin on the event. The feast of Mardi Gras (Fat Tuesday) has become an emblem of the city, and each year people make their way to New Orleans to get their fill of sin before the long weeks of repentance. Women bare their breasts for beads, while drunkards, masked and unmasked, engage in various and sundry acts of debauchery.

But amid all the celebrating one might ask: When did this party begin? It turns out Voodoo isn't the only Crescent City custom that combines Catholic imagery and traditions with pagan rituals and beliefs. To understand Mardi Gras we must go back to the agricultural magic practiced in pre-Christian Europe.

Before Easter—and After

For our ancestors the turning of the seasons was a matter of the utmost urgency. A late spring could mean famine for the entire tribe. To ensure the ice would melt, the beasts would mate, and the plants would bloom once more, ceremonies were performed. By appeasing the gods who held sway over the weather, they hoped to avoid the ever-looming threat of starvation. The gods received offerings and praise. In return, the congregation expected their blessings for the crops and the community. The bigger the ritual, the greater the rewards they could expect, and so these ceremonies involved not only priestly or shamanic castes but people from all walks of life.

In those days seasonal eating wasn't an affectation for foodies; it was mandatory. When the ground was blanketed with snow, there were no more greens to be had. The produce put up after the harvest had to last through the cold, lean months. The frozen ground would produce no more root vegetables and the icy fields gave no more grain. Spring was a cause for celebration and relief. It was a sign you had made it through the winter alive and a promise that your bland winter diet would soon be augmented with fresh fruits and vegetables. And so it was not surprising that these rituals involved a great degree of merriment.

This revelry often took on a decidedly sexual character. This was in part due to the high spirits attendant upon a good party, but there was a deeper meaning as well. Millennia before Freud, our ancestors recognized the connection between the sexual urge and the force that drove the cattle into rutting and set the flowers blooming. They hoped that their own licentiousness could encourage their farms and hunting grounds to mate and produce the resources to keep the village fat and happy through the warm times and well stocked against the inevitable barren months.

By the time of the Roman Empire, these customs were already ancient. The Romans celebrated Lupercalia on February 15 even though they no longer remembered the god or gods to whom it had originally been dedicated. Noble youths clad in loincloths (garb more suited to shepherds and peasants) ran through the streets lashing passersby with whips made of goatskin. Instead of running from these floggings, people (particularly young women) crowded to receive their blows, since they believed they would encourage fertility and easy childbirth. The whole event was marked with much drinking and merrymaking.

After the rise of Christianity some efforts were made to stamp out these heathen customs, but to little avail. The wealthy and educated may have turned up their noses at the local superstitions, but the peasantry weren't about to put their crops at risk—or give up the year's best party! At last the Church bureaucracy decided that if you can't beat them, you might as well join them. As was often their wont, Church officials reinterpreted the tradition in the light of Christian mythology. The holiday that marked the earth's return to life became the Easter feast of Christ's death and resurrection, and the riotous fertility festivals became a last celebration before the austerities of Lent. Since meat was forbidden during that period of purification and mortification, the rites became a last chance at indulgence, a carne vale, or "farewell to the flesh."

The carnival season officially ran from January 6 (the Feast of the Epiphany, when the Three Kings brought their gifts to Jesus) to the Tuesday before Ash Wednesday. Revelers wore masks, which allowed them to gamble, carouse, and break social barriers anonymously. While the festival first became popular in Italy (so popular that Pope Gregory XIII made Mardi Gras an official holiday in 1582), it later spread throughout the Roman Catholic parts of continental Europe.

Then, with the dawn of the colonial era, Carnival spread through much of the New World as well. Portuguese settlers brought the festivities to Brazil and Goa, India. French colonists invited to Trinidad by the Spanish established a carnival tradition that continues to this day. And on March 3, 1699, Lord Iberville and his troops celebrated the holiday by holding the first Mass of record in French Louisiana and naming their campsite (about sixty miles from present-day New Orleans) Point du Mardi Gras.

Mardi Gras Comes to New Orleans

The first official mention of Mardi Gras in New Orleans comes from a 1781 Spanish report that expressed concerns about slaves wearing masks during celebrations. By 1806 masked balls were banned by the New Orleans City Council in an effort to tame the unruly and sometimes violent partying that was already a staple of the city's pre-Lenten celebrations. Alas, the councilors learned that passing a law in the city was one thing, enforcing it quite another. By 1823 masked balls were once again permitted, and by 1827 masked and costumed revelers were once again making their way through the city streets.

From the start Mardi Gras in New Orleans was known for the large number of black and Creole participants. Writing in 1823, a Protestant minister described the proceedings:

"The great Congo-dance is performed. Everything is license and revelry. Some hundreds of negroes, male and female, follow the king of the wake. .

. . All the characters that follow him, of leading estimation, have their peculiar dress, and their own contortions. They dance, and their streamers fly, and the bells that they have hung about them tinkle. Never will you see gayer countenances, demonstrations of more forgetfulness of the past and the future, and more entire abandonment to the joyous existence of the present moment."

This led to many calls for the banning of these pagan rites, especially with the continuing problems of violence and street crime during the celebrations. A solution came from six businessmen who had been involved in similar celebrations in Mobile, Alabama. Forming together as the Mystick Krewe of Comus, they organized a torchlit parade and ball. Comus started many Mardi Gras traditions that are still held today, particularly the floats that throw trinkets to the crowds. Unlike the wild black celebrations, membership in their secret society was limited to white people of the appropriate social class. The only blacks who marched with their floats were hired torch-bearers, and the only blacks at their balls were servants.

But black revelers were not so easily denied their chance at a party. Since 1783 the Perseverance Benevolent and Mutual Aid Association had served as a form of insurance and social aid for free blacks in New Orleans. It would be followed by many other similar groups that would sponsor their own krewes, carnival organizations, and Mardi Gras parties. Membership in these groups meant more than just a ticket to the best balls; it provided a network whereby unemployed or injured laborers could find work and deceased members could be guaranteed a decent burial. While the white krewes marched through the French Quarter, the black krewes made their way through the African American neighborhoods.

Another Mardi Gras tradition would soon arise: the Black Indian "tribes." Since the earliest African presence in the New World, blacks and Indians had interacted. Many maroons (escaped slaves) found a home among the Indian tribes living in the inaccessible swamplands beyond the plantations. To pay tribute for their aid, blacks formed "tribes" or "gangs" named after their neighborhoods. Members of these organizations were known for their intricately beaded costumes, complete with plumage, sparkling rhinestones, and moccasins. The feathers hearkened back to Indian ceremonial costumes, while the beading was inspired by West African artwork. The Indian tribes became especially popular after a New Orleans visit by Buffalo Bill's Wild West Show in 1884.

In the beginning, tribes frequently engaged in turf wars, with regular fights between "uptown" and "downtown" tribes that often devolved into gunfights, hatchet attacks, and stabbings. Since the New Orleans police were generally occupied with keeping order in the white sections of town, these gang wars raged with impunity in the poor black areas. Today the Black Indians remain an important part of Mardi Gras celebrations, but their conflicts are much more ritualized and less bloody. When two tribes pass each other on the street, each "chief" will demand of the other "You humba" (pay your respects to me) and respond "Me no humba, YOU humba." This will then be greeted by a series of war whoops and intricate dance maneuvers. At the end of this display, each will acknowledge the other's skill and the quality of the tribe's costumes. (Some say the cost and skill involved in costume designing contributed to the peace between rival tribes. No one who has spent hundreds of hours and thousands of dollars designing a suit wants to risk ruining it in a fight!)

Another black krewe, formed by the Zulu Social Aid and Pleasure Club, first marched in 1909. Its king wore a lard can as a crown and carried a banana stalk scepter. The Zulus were one of the first krewes to bring in a celebrity king, when Louis Armstrong was accorded the honor in 1949. They are still the lead krewe in the largely black Zulu parade that takes place alongside the historically white Rex parade. The Zulus have attracted some controversy for their grass skirt and blackface costumes, but have risen above that to become one of the most popular and famous Mardi Gras krewes. The organization's choir, the Zulu Ensemble, performs at local churches, gospel concerts, schools, funerals, and the Jazz and Heritage Festival. During the Christmas season Zulus provide baskets to needy families and donate funds and time to various community organizations.

Throws

After putting all that effort into building a fine float and fancy costume, you want to make sure the audience appreciates your handiwork. And as everyone in the Crescent City knows, a little lagniappe (extra free gift) will always win hearts and minds. To that end, "throws"—gifts tossed into the crowd—are an intrinsic part of Mardi Gras parades. (An earlier custom of throwing flour and pepper into the audience wasn't nearly so endearing.)

Sometime in the 1920s, the members of the Rex Krewe acquired a large number of inexpensive glass beads from Czechoslovakia, strung them into necklaces, and threw them from their floats as mementos. They were warmly received by the crowd and thus began a trend that has lived on: Mardi Gras beads. After World War II the beads were imported from Japan, and later, plastic replaced glass and China replaced Japan as the primary supplier. According to Fred Berger, owner of Mardi Gras Imports of Slidell, Louisiana, the average Mardi Gras krewe member spends approximately $800 on beads and "some people won't bat an eye at spending $2,000 or $2,500."

In 1959 New Orleans artist Alvin Sharpe created another famous Mardi Gras tradition: the doubloon. The Rex krewe ordered eighty-three thousand of his intricately detailed aluminium doubloons. Unsure how they would go over, they asked him to leave off the date on all but a few, so that any left over could be used another year. But it turned out that they were a huge hit: between 1960 and 1970 Rex threw 2.75 million doubloons. Others soon followed suit, and today collectors strive to acquire complete collections of their favorite krewes at the parade or at various online and offline memorabilia stores.

Other krewes throw plastic toys or cups emblazoned with their logo. But few gifts are as prized as the Zulu krewe's hand-painted coconuts. Originally the Zulu krewe became famous for throwing "golden nuggets," or gold-painted walnuts. Although these were cheaper than glass beads, they were greatly appreciated by the crowd since they could be eaten while watching the parade or at the tavern afterwards. (Bar owners along the route were less thrilled about the walnut shells that inevitably littered their floor.) Later they began throwing coconuts that were painted gold and decorated with glitter. Most featured the Zulu blackface design, and some even featured hair and hats. After a number of lawsuits from people who were hit by thrown coconuts, the club briefly suspended the practice. But to keep the tradition alive, the Louisiana Legislature passed SB188 (the "Coconut Bill"), excluding the krewe from liability for injuries caused by coconuts handed off (as opposed to tossed) from the float. Over one hundred thousand coconuts are passed out during a typical Zulu parade.

But while the regular coconuts are treasured, those who are especially favored by the Zulus (or who wish to purchase one from their master engraver, Willie Clark) may get one of their special "Mardi Gras Coconuts." These are meticulously decorated and engraved; they may have as many as thirty-seven colors and sixty-eight color mixtures on their surface. As Zulu member Lester Pollard says, "Our organization centers around the coconut—the coconut is everything to us! Man, we've got laws passed concerning our coconuts!"

Kings and Queens

For the 1872 Mardi Gras, the Crescent City had a noble visitor: Grand Duke Alexis Romanoff of Russia. To entertain him, a number of young New Orleans businessmen formed the Rex Organization. Unlike the Comus krewe's nighttime parade, the Rex krewe held their parade during the day. To honor Duke Alexis, they elected one of their members, Lewis Solomon, as king of the parade. Crowned and robed, riding a horse, and holding a scepter he borrowed from a traveling actor, Solomon became the first Rex, King of the Carnival. (He was also the first to march under the purple, green, and gold banner that has become emblematic of the New Orleans festivities.) Following in their lead, many other krewes elected their own kings, queens, and royal courts.

These royals are generally announced on King's Night—the twelfth night after Christmas, also known as the Feast of the Epiphany. While this ostensibly pays homage to the three magi who brought gifts to the Christ child, its roots stretch back to the Roman holiday of Saturnalia. In a sentiment familiar to many Mardi Gras revelers, the Roman poet Lucian had Saturn tell his devotees how to celebrate his party:

"During My week the serious is barred; no business allowed. Drinking, noise and games and dice, appointing of kings and feasting of slaves, singing naked, clapping of frenzied hands, an occasional ducking of corked faces in icy water—such are the functions over which I preside."

During Saturnalia the family festivities were presided over by a Lord of Misrule, who ensured that his subjects were engaging in properly riotous behavior. This office was determined by lot: pieces of cake were passed out among the family, and the one whose cake contained a fava bean was raised to the throne until the festival was over. This is echoed today by the king cake, which is a staple of New Orleans Twelfth Night festivities.

A king cake is a pastry rather like a coffee cake, decorated with purple, gold, and green icing. Each weekend between Twelfth Night and Mardi Gras, slices are passed out at parties. The person whose slice contains a tiny plastic or ceramic baby is crowned king or queen—and is expected to pick up the tab for next week's party! Similar traditions exist in France (gâteau de rois), England

(Twelfth Cakes), Portugal (bolo rei), Greece (vasilopita), and Catalonia (tortell).

Because the Mardi Gras royal offices are highly prestigious and sought after, the Twelfth Night Revelers, one of the oldest krewes, have resorted to yet another time-honored New Orleans tradition: rigging the elections. Instead of a real king cake, a wooden replica is presented at the climax of their ball. To the tune of "Thank Heaven for Little Girls," the debutantes seated in the call-out section are called forward and led to the wooden cake, which has many small boxes. Most of the boxes contain small pieces of cake, and a few contain beans on a chain. The girls who have been chosen to serve as maids in the court receive boxes containing silver beans, and the one who has been chosen as queen is given the box with a gold bean.

The krewes have traditionally been segregated by race, gender, and social status. Popular krewes like Comus, Momus, Rex, and Endymion refused membership to blacks, Jews, Italians, women, and working-class people. Alternate krewes were established catering to these excluded groups, like Zulu (black), the Virgilians (Italian), Iris (female), and Petronius (gay). Even canines had their own society, the Krewe of Barkus! Then, in 1991, the New Orleans City Council demanded the integration of the krewes. A law was passed prohibiting any club, marching society, or parade organization sponsoring public Mardi Gras activities from excluding anyone from membership because of race, color, sex, sexual orientation, national origin, ancestry, age, physical condition, or disability.

In response the old-line Comus, Momus, and Proteus clubs pulled out of the Mardi Gras parades altogether. Others allowed in a handful of minority members, while still others moved their parades out to the largely white suburban parishes. In the end, most of the old krewes—and new multicultural ones like Harry

Connick Jr.'s Krewe of Orpheus—embraced new minority members. "New Orleans is a city that survives on its tourism industry and its reputation for hospitality," Norman C. Francis, president of the largely black Xavier University, explained. "For people around the country to think we were living in isolation, that we were shunning diversity, that would have been our death notice."

TRADITIONS: MUSIC

New Orleans is a party that never ends—and you can't have a party without music! The cultural blending that produced Louisiana's unique cuisine has also given us some of America's most colorful and distinctive tunes. Many of these songs pay homage to the religion and magic of New Orleans, while others discuss the historical events that shaped the Crescent City. If you want to understand the Big Easy, you'll need to learn something about its soundtrack.

To give you some idea of the various influences on New Orleans music, consider legendary Cajun fiddler Dennis McGee. His grandfather was an Irish immigrant, and his mother was half Seminole Indian. (He still insisted McGee was a French name, since "I don't know anyone named McGee who doesn't speak French.") He performed on some of the first recordings of Cajun music with Amédé Ardoin, a Creole singer and accordion player. Later he recorded many duets with his brother-inlaw, violinist and furniture salesman Sady Courville.

Still another example is the New Orleans pianist and composer Louis Moreau Gottschalk. Born in 1829 to a Jewish businessman from London and a refugee from Saint-Domingue, young Gottschalk began teaching himself to play piano at the tender age of three. Schooled in Europe, he would later incorporate the French, Spanish, and African rhythms of his native city into compositions like "Bamboula!" and "The Banjo." Upon the elder Gottschalk's early death, Louis took responsibility for his five half-siblings by his father's quadroon mistress. Touring ceaselessly, he played to adoring audiences throughout South America until his death in Brazil in 1869.

New Orleans has always been a place of commingling musical styles. At a time when few American cities had one opera company, New Orleans had several. A visitor could hear Chopin played at a conservatory during the day, then listen to bawdy ragtime and barrelhouse at a local speakeasy or brothel at night. All these influences came together to create several styles of music that have become symbolic of the Big Easy in all its high-living, hard-partying glory.

Delta Blues

In Islamic West Africa, griots (or female griottes) preserve history and culture through their music. Accompanying themselves on stringed instruments, they sing tales of ancestors and their feats and ribald tunes about love and its various complications. Although their presence is required at celebrations and rituals, the griots frequently occupy a liminal place in their society. Admired for their talent and sometimes paid handsomely for their performances, they are also often shunned as sorcerers and men and women of dubious moral character. While some also hold day jobs in their community, others support themselves as traveling musicians, making their living by their voice and their instrument.

The stringed instruments used by the griots resemble the guitar and banjo commonly found in African American folk music. The griot melodies are based on a pentatonic scale—instead of the seven notes (Do, Re, Mi, etc.) found in a major scale, melodies are based on scales of five notes. The third and fifth notes of these scales are often flattened, played at a pitch below "just intonation" (equal divisions between each note of the scale). The griots frequently improvise on standard tunes, making up new lyrics on the spot to honor generous patrons or mock stingy ones.

These musical conventions can be found among the descendants of slaves brought from West Africa. Many blues songs are based on a pentatonic scale, and whenever flattened thirds and fifths appear in American music, they are generally called blue notes. In African American society blues artists have often held a place very like that of the griots. They provide entertainment for their audiences, and a lucky few can even earn a living at it—but many have also gained a reputation for heavy drinking, promiscuity, and drug use. And a few have even been accused of sorcery. Robert Johnson's legendary "deal with the Devil" at the crossroads is one example, but many other blues musicians have had reputations as "conjures" or "Hoodoo men."

Like griots, blues singers preserve the lives and cultures of their people. Their music could often be bawdy, with surprisingly frank discussions of sexuality. Blues musicians would brag about their sexual prowess (Skip James's "All Night Long") or complain about their impotence (Robert Johnson's "Dead Shrimp Blues"). Partners were lauded for their fidelity, or more often criticized for their cheating ways. But blues music also chronicled the lives of hardscrabble farmers and day laborers under Jim Crow. The blues gave a voice to anonymous convicts on the chain gang and celebrated legendary gangsters like "Stagger" Lee. It spoke of gin joints and prisons, of cotton fields and factories, of winning hands and hard times. And it described, often and in loving detail, the temptations, tribulations, and magic one might find in New Orleans and the surrounding countryside.

In 1925 Gertrude "Ma" Rainey sang in "Louisiana Hoodoo Blues," Going to the Louisiana bottom to get me a hoodoo hand Going to the Louisiana bottom to get me a hoodoo hand Gotta stop these women from taking my man.

Later, male blues singers like Alger "Texas" Alexander and George "Little Hat" Jones followed in her footsteps, traveling to the Crescent City to win back their lady love with a mojo bag prepared by some of the best Hoodoo doctors in the South. New

Orleans was a place where the broken-hearted might find love magic—or, more precisely, the power to make a wandering lover return. The blues were more a feature of the rural delta than urban New Orleans. Most blues songs about New Orleans are sung by outsiders looking to visit for business or pleasure.

One classic blues saga, "House of the Rising Sun," began as a Kentucky folk tune. Told by a young woman brought to New Orleans and forced into prostitution (or, in other versions, a dissipate gambling man on his last legs), this archetypal tale of sin without salvation cast New Orleans in the role of Sodom on the Mississippi—a role that would have been all too familiar, and alluring, to folk growing up on the frontier and dreaming of city life. Like many a blues song, "Rising Sun" wagged its finger at sin while making it as attractive as possible. Grand Ole Opry founder Roy Acuff made a recording of this folk standard that became a country classic, and in 1948 Huddie "Leadbelly" Ledbetter gave us his version in one of his last studio sessions. Later other black musicians like Nina Simone and Miriam Makeba reclaimed this song in a blue mode.

A soulful rendition by the Animals topped the charts on both sides of the Atlantic in 1964. This version combined blues riffs with electronic instrumentation and vocal stylings reminiscent of the untrained singers of the Delta blues. This combination had for several years fueled the development of a movement that took its name from an old blues euphemism for sexual intercourse: rock and roll. A whole new generation came to know New Orleans as a hospice where morals and good character could die in a suitably entertaining fashion. But this was hardly the first time blues had shaped popular music—or vice versa. Generations before, New Orleans had seen another movement wherein West African song styles and scales had met contemporary standards and formed a new, enduring music that attained worldwide popularity.

Dixieland Jazz

In 1896 a young New Orleans newsboy named Emile "Stale Bread" Lacoumbe attracted attention (and newspaper sales) with his virtuoso harmonica playing. Gathering a troupe of young musicians around him, he soon gave up the newspaper business for a life as leader of Stale Bread's Spasm Band. At first they played on soapbox guitars and washtub bass fiddles, but as they attracted attention they added cornets, clarinets, and other store-bought instruments to their instrumentation. Whooping and hollering in time with their songs, they soon became a local sensation and played at many local taverns, theaters, and brothels.

Then in 1905, Jack Robinson, owner of the Haymarket Restaurant, hired a band of experienced musicians to copy the sound of Stale Bread's street urchins, a group he billed as the Razzy Dazzy Spasm Band. Alas, the original Spasm band took umbrage at their competition and protested by heaving rocks and bricks through the Haymarket's windows. To placate them, Robinson quickly repainted his placards to feature the Razzy Dazzy Jazzy Band—one of the first recorded usages of the word jazz.

Other historians date the beginning of jazz to 1898 and the end of the Spanish-American War. As military bands returned from Cuba and decommissioned, the city was flooded with used band instruments. Black musicians who had hitherto been unable to afford cornets, tubas, and trombones quickly bought up these and other bargain-priced instruments and taught themselves how to play.

These self-taught musicians used unconventional playing techniques and developed unusual renderings of popular tunes.

They also incorporated the complex rhythms of African musical traditions. Where most brass bands of the time emphasized the first and third beats of a measure, African music tended to concentrate on the backbeats—resulting in a distinctive oom-PAH oom-PAH sound. Since many were unable to read sheet music, they generally learned tunes by ear, rehearsing together until they achieved the desired sound. And since these ensembles frequently changed personnel, their tunes tended to be more loosely structured and improvisational than traditional brass band music.

Soon many white bands were emulating the sounds and techniques of the New Orleans jazz bands. As the recording industry dawned, many promoters hired white bands to play sanitized versions of popular New Orleans tunes, then released them for a nationwide audience. The first jazz hit, 1917's "Livery Stable Blues" by a white group called the Original Dixieland Jazz Band, had little of the ragged rhythm and free-form improvisation that marked the best of New Orleans jazz. Still, it went on to sell over a million copies.

Not until 1922 would a black jazz band be featured on record, when Louisiana trombonist Edward "Kid" Ory recorded "Ory's Creole Trombone" in a Los Angeles studio. Later Ory moved to Chicago, where he played alongside New Orleans jazz legends like cornetist Joe "King" Oliver. Meanwhile another trumpet player from the poor side of New Orleans was making his name in dance halls and riverboats—Louis "Satchmo" Armstrong. Raised by his beloved grandmother, a conjure woman, Armstrong maintained a healthy respect and fear of Voodoo throughout his life. Many of his peers whispered that he, like Robert Johnson, owed much of his success to bargains with supernatural powers.

Another legendary jazz pioneer, pianist Ferdinand "Jelly Roll" Morton, was also deeply involved in Voodoo. In a 1938 interview with folklorist Alan Lomax, Morton described how notorious killer Aaron Harris was able to avoid prosecution despite his many crimes, thanks to a Hoodoo woman named Madame Papaloos:

Madame Papaloos is supposed, that is . . . from certain evidences, to tumble up Aaron's house. Take all the sheets off the bed. Tumble the mattresses over. Put sheets in front of the glasses. Take chairs and tumble 'em all over. That is said and known to . . . discourage the judge from prosecuting.

"And . . . of course the different witnesses . . . have all their tongues supposed to be tied. They supposed to tie 'em with . . . lambs' tongues. And . . . beef tongues and veal tongues out of the markets. And stick 'em full of needles. That is what I understand. I don't know, 'cause I've never seen 'em stick pins and needles all through 'em. And take some . . . we'll say twine in order to make it real secure. And tie these tongues up.

And that's supposed to have the prosecuting attorneys and the judges and the jurors and so forth and so on, have their tongues tied that they can't talk against whoever the victim's supposed to be. Not the victim, but

. . . the one that's arrested, the prisoner. So Aaron Harris was always successful in getting out of all of his troubles."

Morton was raised by his godmother, conjure woman and Voodoo Priestess Laura Hunter. But although their relationship was by all accounts a loving one, Morton always feared she had sold his soul to the Devil and that he would die soon after she did. When she passed on in 1940, Morton told several of his close friends that his time had come. A few months later he died of heart failure.

Unfortunately for the New Orleans jazz scene, its best black musicians (like many other black citizens) were joining the exodus north to Chicago and other Midwestern cities, where well-paying factory work was easy to come by. Ory made a name for himself in California; Armstrong became a sensation in Chicago and later New York City. During the Great Depression even the best musicians found it difficult to earn a living with their instruments. Kid Ory put down his trombone and took up chicken farming, while King Oliver worked at a roadside fruit stand, and legendary clarinetist Sidney Bechet opened a tailor shop in Harlem after gigs for his New Orleans Feetwarmers dried up.

When the economy improved, interest in Dixieland jazz returned, but traditional players faced new competition from swing, big band, and later bebop players. Dixieland jazz was seen by many new performers as old-fashioned and stodgy. Louis Armstrong's charismatic stage patter was disparaged by some young black musicians as "Uncle Tomming" for a white audience. New Orleans jazz became yet another tourist attraction for visitors, as sanitized and preserved as a ride at Disneyworld. In the words of eminent jazz critic Gary Giddins:

"Some of the music froze in a kind of Dixieland wax museum, complete with straw hat and sleeve garter, as compared to the original innovators, who were usually dressed to the nines—like hustlers, gamblers, sharp- looking guys. Somehow a culture of John Stetson hats and tailored threads was transformed into a culture of beer and peanuts and garters and vests, playing the same goddamn tunes every night. When it is done well that kind of music can still be electrifying But more often, it has become a predictable exercise."

But while time may have passed much Dixieland jazz by, it influenced yet another style of music that has become indelibly connected with the sound of New Orleans.

Zydeco

One popular Louisiana folk song, "Les Haricots Sont Pas Salés" ("The Snap Beans Aren't Salty"), describes hard times when the larder is empty and you can't even afford salt pork to spice up the beans. In the local dialect, les haricots (pronounced "lay zarico") became le zydeco. When it was recorded by Clifton Chenier in 1965, his bluesy, soulful version became a regional hit and gave its name to a whole new genre of music—zydeco. But this new sensation had deep roots in Louisiana Creole—and a pedigree stretching back to the first African slaves and Acadian settlers.

In the remote bayous and swamps, the Cajuns had to entertain themselves. Many learned to play music, making their own fiddles and stomping and clapping to provide rhythm at dance festivals. Since illiteracy was common, stories and legends were often passed down through ballads and songs. But though they were isolated, the Cajuns were not alone. Their songs were influenced by the music of neighboring blacks and various European immigrants. All would come together at house parties where musicians played till the wee hours of the night for a whooping and hollering audience.

African call-and-response informed the Cajun tradition of vocal improvisation. Juré, the syncopated field songs of black workers, added rhythmic complexity to the Cajun reels and two-steps. After World War II, rhythm and blues music inspired black and white musicians, and horn sections and electric guitars ultimately became part of many Cajun and Creole bands. Country music and Western swing had a similar influence, introducing pedal steel guitars to many lineups. But two instruments became particularly associated with zydeco.

When Germans arrived in New Orleans, they brought accordions with them. At first Cajun musicians shunned the new instrument. Its musical range was more limited than the violin, and it was tuned in keys that did not match well with the tunings used by Cajun fiddlers. By about 1925 accordion makers began producing instruments tuned in C and D—keys that were often used in Cajun songs. Although the accordion was not as versatile as the fiddle, it could be played more loudly, and its sound carried well through even the most rambunctious crowd. The accordion soon became part of the region's signature sound.

Folk musicians have long used washboards not only to clean their clothes but as a rhythm instrument. By tapping the washboard or scraping its ridged surface, a washboard player can produce a backbeat and emphasize particular passages. Traditionally an actual washboard is used. But in the late 1940s Cleveland Chenier (Clifton's brother) had a specially modified instrument produced by a local tinsmith. This board dispensed with the wooden frame, producing a distinctive rasp. Soon other musicians were hanging these vests frottoirs (vests for rubbing) around their necks and playing them by running spoons, bottle openers, or thimbles across their ridged surface.

In the 1950s the Chenier Brothers burst out of Opelousas, Louisiana, with "Hey, 'Tite Fille" ("Hey, Little Girl"). Signed to blues label Chess Records, their peppy, infectious grooves attracted nationwide attention from blues and jazz fans. Combining Cajun music with influences from musicians like Fats Domino and Professor Longhair, they helped to make zydeco a national phenomenon. Clifton Chenier won a Grammy Award in 1983 for his album I'm Here! In 1989, two years after his death, he was inducted into the Blues Hall of Fame.

Perhaps the most popular zydeco artist is Stanley Dural Jr., better known by his stage name, Buckwheat Zydeco. From 1971 to 1976 Dural led a funk band, then decided to concentrate on traditional Louisiana music, which his father, accordionist Stanley Sr., had played back in the 1940s and '50s, when it was called "la la."

Trading in his Hammond organ for an accordion, Dural became the frontman for the Ils Sont Partis (They're Off!) band. Adding funky grooves to traditional zydeco, Buckwheat Zydeco signed a major deal with Island Records. Later he toured with Eric Clapton and Willie Nelson and contributed tunes to movies like The Big Easy and to national commercials for Lincoln Mercury, Toyota, Cheerios, and Budweiser.

Today a number of bands carry on the zydeco tradition. Experienced musicians like Grammy winner Ida Lewis "Queen Ida" Guillory and C. J. Chenier (Clifton Chenier's son) play alongside newcomers like Keith Frank and the Soileau Zydeco Band and twelve-year-old accordionist Guyland Leday. Chris Ardoin carries on the tradition started by his ancestors Amédé and Alphonse "Bois Sec" Ardoin, but adds a touch of hiphop to the mix. Geno Delafose gives a nod to country and western in his "nouveau zydeco." In paying tribute to zydeco's roots while incorporating new influences, all these musicians continue to reflect New Orleans—a city that has always been quick to mix and match the traditional and the modern.

TRADITIONS: FOOD

New Orleans is legendary for its unique cuisine, and foodies from around the world come to the Big Easy to do some big eating. Well-heeled epicures can go to famous establishments like Brennan's, Commander's Palace, and Antoine's to feast on deliciously decadent culinary delights. Those on more modest budgets can enjoy beignets and chicory coffee or nosh on buttery-sweet pecan pralines after a hearty bowl of jambalaya or some dirty rice at one of the city's many less fancy but no less satisfying restaurants. While New Orleans caters to all seven of the deadly sins, gluttons will find the Crescent City a particularly delightful stop on their travels.

Beyond the sensual pleasures of a good repast, there are many lessons to be learned in the culinary history of New Orleans. The tale of any civilization can be told at its table, and many legends and interesting facts can be found behind the meals and beverages that make New Orleans a gourmand's paradise. If we're going to study New Orleans Voodoo, let us take a side trip through some New Orleans kitchens. The results may stimulate your intellect and will certainly stimulate your appetite.

Jambalaya

According to one story, this classic New Orleans dish originated when a hungry traveler showed up late one night at an inn. Alas, the innkeeper, Jean, told him that nothing was left. Undeterred, the traveler told him "Jean, balayez!" ("Jean, sweep something together!") The innkeeper complied, and was so delighted by the rice-based mix of available scraps and leftovers that he named the dish "Jean balayez." Others claim the name derives from the word jambon (ham in French) and ya (purportedly an African word for rice), while still others claim it dates from the Spanish occupation of New Orleans and is a portmanteau of jamón (Spanish for ham) and paella, the famous Spanish rice dish.

Perhaps the most plausible explanation comes from culinary scholar Andrew Sigal. He notes that ham is not a particularly prominent ingredient in most jambalayas, and that pilau au jambon or paella con jamón would be a more likely name for these dishes in French or Spanish. But in the Provençal dialect of French there is a word that describes a mishmash or a rabble and also describes a stew of rice, vegetables, and various meats—jambalaia. But while the word's origins may be European, the spicy seasonings that are common to many New Orleans jambalayas show a definite African influence. Ceebu jën, a popular Senegalese dish, combines tomatoes, rice, fish, and vegetables with abundant amounts of hot chile peppers. When meat is used instead of, or in addition to, fish, the dish is known as Wolof Rice (after the Wolof people of modern-day Senegal) and is served throughout Western Africa. Its fiery flavor has been preserved in Louisiana, where many like their jambalayas hot and some like them even hotter.

Just about every cook in Louisiana has the recipe for the One True Jambalaya and will swear that everyone else's is just a pale imitation. Creole (or red) jambalaya includes tomatoes and tomato paste, while Cajun (brown) jambalaya shuns tomatoes and gets its brown coloration from the bits of browned meat scraped from the bottom of the pan. The other ingredients used will vary. Cajun cooks typically include andouille, or smoked sausage, while Creole cooks generally add shrimp, but after that just about everything is fair game. Jambalaya can be made with chicken, boar, shrimp, fish, crawfish, alligator, beef, or just about any other meat you have around the larder. Onions and bell peppers are generally sautéed along with the meats and other vegetables. Stock is then added along with rice and, near the end, fast-cooking items like shrimp or crawfish. Cayenne pepper and Tabasco sauce are often added, although some prefer milder jambalaya.

Jambalaya became especially well known after the release of the 1952 Hank Williams Sr. hit "Jambalaya." Taking the melody to a classic Cajun tune, "Grand Texas," Williams added new lyrics celebrating life on the bayou, where one could enjoy "Jambalaya, a-crawfish pie and-a file gumbo." His version of the Cajun classic reached number one on the country music charts and remains one of Williams's most popular tunes. And when Luisah Teish wanted to name her now-classic 1988 collection of African-inspired women's charms and rituals, the most evocative title she could think of was Jambalaya.

Gumbo

Like Texas chili and New England clam chowder, gumbo has become an emblem (some would even say a cliché) of the Crescent City table. Gumbo has a long history: in 1803 it was served at a gubernatorial reception in New Orleans, and in 1804 the dish made an appearance at a Cajun gathering. When Robert Tallant and Lyle Saxon compiled their leftover tales of New Orleans history and folklore, they called it Gumbo Ya-Ya. But what exactly is gumbo anyway?

At its simplest, gumbo is a thick soup served over rice. This soup most often contains vegetables along with some kind of meat or seafood. In 1832 Théodore Pavie wrote about consuming squirrel gumbo (which he described as a "delicious stew") during his journey to Louisiana and Texas, while other writers have described owl and muskrat gumbo. Today the most common gumbos are seafood gumbo (which generally contains some combination of oysters, shrimp, crawfish, and crab) and chicken and andouille sausage gumbo. The "holy trinity" of Louisiana cooking—diced celery, onions, and bell peppers—is often included, and bay leaves and cayenne pepper are commonly used for seasoning. But what separates a gumbo from a mere soup is the thickening agent.

One of the most common thickeners comes from Africa: okra. Many people loathe its slimy texture, but properly cooked okra is not only delicious but also good for you. Okra is high in vitamin B6 and fiber. It helps stabilize blood sugar, as it curbs the rate at which sugar is absorbed from the intestinal tract, and helps ensure intestinal health, while its mucilage binds cholesterol and bile-acid- carrying toxins and helps feed probiotics. That mucilage—called "slime" by those who dislike okra—also thickens many gumbos. In Africa hearty okra soups are an integral part of many West African diets, and the plant that Kongo peoples call quingombo or ngombo has given its name to Louisiana's signature dish.

But the other classic gumbo thickener comes not from Africa but from the Choctaw Indians. After their soups were done cooking, they would throw in a pinch of finely ground dried sassafras leaves. This thickened the broth and added a spicy herbal flavor and aroma reminiscent of eucalyptus. The settlers came to call this filé powder and used it in their gumbos. But while okra had to be boiled to release its mucilage, filé powder could be added only after the gumbo had been removed from the heat lest it turn the dish into a gluey, stringy mess. Today gumbos are thickened either with filé or okra, but never both. Traditionally seafood gumbos are made with okra while gumbos made with game are thickened with filé (since okra was not available during the fall and winter hunting seasons).

Those who can't get over their okra prejudices and who can't find filé needn't despair. In addition to Indian and African thickeners,

New Orleans cooks often rely on a French roux. Combining equal parts flour and oil or butter, they whisk the combination over high heat until it begins to darken. This produces a rich, nutty flavor but requires patience: a roux-in-progress must be whisked constantly lest it burn and become unpalatable. Some Cajun cooks will keep a dark roux cooking for nearly an hour, whisking away all the while.

And vegetarians and even vegans can get in on the gumbo game by making a traditional New Orleans Good Friday dish, gumbo z'herbes. Catholics traditionally celebrate Good Friday by fasting and abstaining from meat. This gumbo is made by combining a variety of different greens—seven, nine, or fifteen, depending on whom you ask. (Tradition says that the number of greens you use will be the number of new friends you make in the coming year.) They are slow-simmered and then drained, reserving the cooking liquid. The pot liquor (reserved liquid) is used to cook rice, and the simmered greens are added to a mix of dark roux and the ever-popular onion, celery, and bell pepper. The greens are then served over a bed of the green rice, giving you a fast that many would call a feast!

Pralines

Not only was he a noted seventeenth-century French diplomat, warrior, and statesman, César de Choiseul du Plessis-Praslin was a great lover of almonds and sweet things. To oblige Plessis-Praslin, his chef, Clement Lassagne, came up with a special recipe—almonds coated with caramelized sugar. These delicacies were popular with Plessis-Praslin's friends as a digestive aid, and were especially loved by the ladies. Recognizing a good thing when he tasted one, Plessis-Praslin grew rich investing in sugar. Chef Lassagne showed a similar flair for business. Upon retiring from his master's employment, he opened a shop in Montargis,

France, entitled Maison de la Prasline and became a wealthy man too.

In 1751 Jesuit missionaries planted sugarcane in what is now downtown New Orleans (their Immaculate Conception Jesuit Church still stands on 130 Baronne Street). At first production was modest at best, as sugarcane is very susceptible to the frosts that occasionally occur even in steamy Louisiana. But by 1795 Etienne de Bore, with expert advice from Antoine Morin, a Saint-Domingue sugar maker, succeeded in producing one hundred thousand pounds (forty-five thousand kilos) of sugar, earning him a $12,000 profit. The Louisiana sugarcane industry was under way—and the subsequent arrival of former plantation owners from Saint-Domingue after the Haitian Revolution only encouraged its growth.

But while sugar was widely available, almonds were more difficult to come by. In their stead, confectioners turned to North America's only native tree nut. During the fall and winter season, these nuts had provided a major food source for Native American tribes, including the Algonquins, who called them pecans. After combining pecans and caramel, they then went one step further than Lassagne by adding heavy cream and butter. The result was a rich, sweet, crunchy confection that has become a favorite New Orleans delicacy—pralines.

During the nineteenth century, pralines became a cottage industry for pralinières, women who sold their pralines on the streets of the French Quarter. Today a number of praline specialty shops offer their wares to tourists and locals throughout that area. Laura's Candies (established in 1913) sells its sweets at 331 Chartres Street, while the Evans Creole Candy Factory (established in 1900) has a shop at 848 Decatur Street, down the street from Aunt Sally's Praline Shop (established in 1930) at 810 Decatur.

Sailors and businesspeople visiting New Orleans brought these treats back home with them, and before long similar candies could be found throughout the Gulf Coast and the southeastern United States. But epicures know that the best pralines can be found in the Crescent City. Nonnatives are cautioned that they are "prah-leans," which have "pihcahns" as one of their major ingredients. Mispronouncing this will forever mark you as an outsider. "Pray-lean" is something one does against a church wall, while "pee-cans" are something one keeps by the bedside.

While the basic praline recipe is simple enough—sugar, pecans, cream, and butter—there is considerable variation in the finished product. Some confectioners make thin, flat pralines filled with pecan bits; others turn out great dollops of creamy goodness with pecan halves inside. Some gild the lily by adding further flavorings to the basic recipe, like shredded coconut, rum, vanilla, chocolate, sweet potato, or peanut butter: Aunt Sally's has even combined two seemingly disparate local favorites in a Tabasco-spiked praline! But most New Orleanians and visitors feel there's no improving on perfection; they like their sweet pecan-studded decadence just the way it is.

Coffee with Chicory

Fearful of the Royal Navy's strength, Napoleon decided to defeat Britain through economic means. In 1806 he banned the import of British goods into French- controlled countries, hoping to starve out the "nation of shopkeepers" and destroy the British economy. But while Napoleon's blockade caused some hardship to English merchants, it caused even more suffering to French coffee lovers. As their beloved beverage became increasingly scarce, they stretched out their java with roasted chicory. But even after the Little Emperor was exiled to St. Helena, his erstwhile subjects continued to drink "café à chicorée," believing that it mellowed the drink and improved the taste.

Creole settlers in the Louisiana Territory had long supplemented their expensive imported coffee with chicory and were only too happy to continue after their beverage of choice became fashionable in France. Then, during the Civil War, Union naval blockades cut off the Confederacy's supply of caffeine. Forced to make do, Confederate civilians and soldiers followed Louisiana's lead and utilized roasted wild chicory root. But after the South's surrender at Appomattox, most Southerners turned their backs on chicory and returned to consuming their coffee neat. The citizens of New Orleans, however, upheld French tradition and continued to drink their bittersweet coffee-chicory brew.

The French believed that the chicory added to coffee served as a contrastimulant, and not entirely without reason. Chicory contains no caffeine, so a chicory admixture is less stimulating than pure coffee and easier on the digestive system. A 1940 study found that two of the compounds found in roasted chicory root, lactucin and lactucopicrin, are mild sedatives that counter the effects of caffeine in rabbits and mice. Herbalists have prescribed chicory root decoctions as a general appetite stimulant and liver tonic, and for jaundice, liver enlargement, gout, and rheumatism. So chicory coffee may be that rarest of items—a New Orleans culinary delight that is actually good for you!

New Orleans chicory coffee is traditionally served au lait, mixed half and half with hot milk. This combination was popularized largely by Café du Monde, which has been catering to tourists and locals from its shop in the French Market (1039 Decatur Street) since 1862. Along with their beignets (fried dough squares dusted with powdered sugar), their café au lait has become a New Orleans tradition for breakfast or any other time. The store is open twenty-four hours a day, seven days a week, except for

Christmas and during hurricane warnings. And if you can't make it to the Big Easy, don't panic. The shop's coffee-chicory blend is available in many supermarkets. (It has also become popular with

Louisiana's growing Vietnamese community, who combine it with condensed milk for their legendary Vietnamese drip coffee.)

Today, New Orleans is the number one coffee port in the country. In 1995, around 241,000 tons of green coffee beans came into New Orleans; that's 27.8 percent of the coffee that entered the United States that year. And New Orleans may also be the origin of another great American tradition. Writing in 1928, Lyle Saxon stated:

It is no unusual thing for a business man to say casually: "Well, let's go and get a cup of coffee," as a visitor in his office is making ready to depart. It is a little thing perhaps, this drinking of coffee at odd times, but it is very characteristic of the city itself. Men in New Orleans give more thought to the business of living than men in other American cities. . . . I have heard Northern business men complain bitterly about these little interruptions for coffee or whatnot.

While we cannot say for certain that the coffee break originated in the Crescent City, it is an interesting hypothesis, and one that deserves careful consideration—preferably over several café au laits and a plate of beignets!

Crawfish

According to Thibodeaux Comeaux, a rice farmer living in Ville Platte, Louisiana, crawfish have only been around since the latter part of the eighteenth century:

You see, people up in Nova Scotia really liked lobster. So it was only natural that when the Acadians made their move to South Louisiana, they brought their Lobster with them. The problem was that the lobsters lost their appetite along the way and shrunk up quite a bit. Since this smaller lobster didn't really look like a lobster any more, the Acadians, now known as Cajuns, called this small crustacean a Crawfish.

Biologists, alas, disagree with M. Comeaux. They say the crawfish is a freshwater decapod crustacean related to the lobster, but one that has been found in the bayous since time immemorial. But scholars and Cajuns alike can agree on one thing: when it comes to good eating, there's nothing quite like the sweet, delicate flavor of crawfish meat. Crawfish boil, crawfish pie, crawfish étouffée, crawfish gumbo, crawfish sausage—all these and more can be made with Louisiana's state crustacean. Yet until recently crawfish were considered a dish only fit for poor bayou dwellers and a few brave souls who wanted to go slumming with the Cajuns. The fine folk in New Orleans would have turned up their noses at any restaurant that would dare put "mudbugs" on its menu.

Attitudes changed after the Great Depression, when improved transportation and cold storage allowed crawfish harvests to reach markets in New Orleans and Baton Rouge. Once they got a taste of fresh crawfish, the city dwellers knew what they had been missing. And as the demand grew, Cajun fishing folk worked diligently to meet the supply. Rice farmers began reflooding their paddies after harvest to produce crawfish for harvest during the autumn, winter, and early spring. This practice of crawfish farming eventually spread to closed- in woodlands and marshland as well. Crawfish farming allowed a more consistent supply of crawfish, as wild harvests varied widely, with years of abundant crawfish separated by years when the crustacean was difficult to come by. As crawfish became more readily available, the markets grew even greater.

By the mid-1960s, the amount of land devoted to crawfish farming had increased to approximately 10,000 acres of managed ponds. At this point, an industry based on peeling crawfish became established, and the new markets for crawfish meat allowed both crawfish farming and wild harvests to increase even more. Today more than 1,600 Louisiana farmers produce crawfish in approximately 120,000 acres of ponds, with over 800 commercial fishers harvesting crawfish from natural wetlands. Their combined annual yield ranges from 75 million to 105 million pounds—over 90 percent of the domestic crop! More than 7,000 people depend directly or indirectly on the crawfish industry, and it is estimated to add over $120 million each year to Louisiana's economy.

But this industry has faced a number of threats. By mid-1997, some 80 percent of the frozen crawfish sold in America were coming from private farmers in Jiangsu Province, China. Louisiana's crawfish industry took its case to Washington, where Senator John Breaux argued, "Crawfish to Louisiana is like cars in Detroit—it's very important to our economy and our culture, and we must do whatever is necessary to preserve the industry." Tariffs ranging between 97 percent and 202 percent were placed on the Chinese imports after the International Trade Commission found that "to upset the crawfish industry would not only put thousands of Louisianans out of work, but it would seriously jeopardize a way of life for a culture."

Today the crawfish industry is still struggling to recover from the damage wrought to the bayous and farms after Katrina. The hurricane sent waves of saltwater into the region, devastating the freshwater-loving crawfish. But though times remain tough, Louisiana's crawfishers remain unbowed. "If there's any industry that'll come back, it's the seafood industry," says Ewell Smith, executive director of the Louisiana Seafood Promotion and Marketing Board. "We've been down before. Katrina is the biggest blow we've ever faced, but we'll come back."

THE SPIRITS

The lois (spirits) of New Orleans were not historically served with vévés, the beautiful cornmeal drawings that are used in Haiti. Instead they were honored with images of the saints and with prayers that were inspired by Roman Catholicism but with the addition of certain phrases and nuances. These would go undetected by outsiders but carried hidden meanings to those who knew their secrets.

Papa La-Bas

In Haiti Papa Legba is recognized as the guardian of the gate. Houngans and mambos believe that no lwa can come down without Legbas approval, and so he is saluted at the beginning of every fete (party) in order that the spirits may arrive and give their blessings. But while he is always given his due, he receives far less attention than some of the more popular lwa. Ghede's party is always one of the year's biggest and rowdiest festivals, and Ogou regularly receives offerings of rum and promises of marriage from women, while both Freda and Danto are pursued by men hoping to win their favor. Atibon Legba (Good Old Legba), by contrast, gets little but his regular offerings of cane syrup, rum, and an occasional rooster.

Outside Haiti the Master of the Crossroads is a far more popular fellow. Legba has become one of the most well known of the lwa, appearing in Grant Morrison's comic book series The Invisibles and William Gibson's science fiction novel Count Zero, and saluted in song by the Talking Heads and Elton John, among others. He has also long been an integral part of conjure and Hoodoo—and while many of the other lwa did not arrive in New

Orleans until much later, Legba (under several different names) has been there all along, waiting by the roadside and opening the door for the spiritual activity that has made the Crescent City so famous.

St. Peter, Papa Limba, and Papa La-Bas

St. Peter, you hold the keys to the gates of the Celestial Kingdom; you open the door to those who are worthy and hold it fast against all others. Open the way for me so that I may partake of the blessings of heaven and shut out those who seek to do harm to me and to mine. Guide me that I may walk upon the road of righteousness and keep me from the wide and easy path that leads to perdition. May you who have known doubt lead me to certainty; may you who have known failure lead me to success.

In 1946 an octogenarian black woman named Josephine Green told Robert Tallant of the time her mother had seen Marie Laveau leading a procession.

All the people wit' her was hollerin' and screamin', "We is goin' to see Papa Limba! We is goin' to see Papa Limba!" My grandpa go runnin' after my ma then, yellin' at her, "You come on in here, Eunice! Don't you know Papa Limba is the devil?" But after that my Ma find out that Papa Limba meant St. Peter and her pa was just foolin' her.

Others have called this figure Liba, Laba, or Papa La-Bas (Papa Over-There). Not only did his name hearken back to the Haitian keeper of the crossroads, but so did one of his favorite songs:

St. Peter, St. Peter, open the door I'm callin' you, come to me!

*St. Peter, St. Peter, open the door*2

Compare this to the second verse of the Priye Gineh, the prayer that opens every Vodou fete:

St. Pierre, ouvrez la porte

St. Pierre, ouvrez la porte, la porte

St. Pierre, ouvrez la porte, la porte du paradis (St. Peter, open the door

St. Peter, open the door, the door

St. Peter, open the door, the door to paradise)

While today Papa Legba is most frequently represented in Haiti by the lame beggar St. Lazarus, in the past he was more often represented by St. Peter. According to Christian mythology, Peter holds the "keys to the kingdom" and is charged with letting the righteous into heaven while keeping the less-than- virtuous out. The similarity between his role and Legba's seemed obvious to practitioners in both Port-au-Prince and New Orleans, so it is not surprising that they would use his image in serving the Old Man at the Crossroads.

But while St. Peter is generally seen as a stern but fair judge (except, perhaps, by those whose names do not appear on the celestial invite list), the Old Man at the Crossroads is famous for his sometimes brutal sense of humor. The African spirits of the crossroads are tricksters who love to sow chaos and strife, messengers who revel in misdirection and mistranslation. Papa La-Bas is by and large a kindly spirit who opens the gate for those who propitiate him. But he also has a mischievous streak and would happily lead astray the gullible, the pompous, and those who need to be taught a lesson.

A close study of St. Peter's life reveals many contradictions and interesting twists. He was "the rock" on which Jesus built his church—but he was also given to moments of wavering faith, nearly drowning when he doubted his ability to walk on water and denying Christ three times after his arrest. And while the Old Man at the Crossroads has sometimes been mistaken for the Devil, St. Peter has been symbolized by that image beloved of metalheads the world over—the inverted cross. (According to legend, he asked to be crucified head down because he was not worthy to die in the same manner as Jesus.) Like the spirit he represents in Haiti and New Orleans—and in Guatemala, where he is syncretized with the chthonic crossroads deity Maximón—St. Peter is a complex and ambiguous figure; it's not surprising that he wound up guarding heaven's doorway.

If you want to work with Papa La-Bas, you can start with an image of St. Peter. These are widely available in botanicas or Catholic supply stores. Images with Peter holding keys are preferred, since they represent his role as heaven's gatekeeper. When you are moving into a new house you can put a St. Peter image above your inside front door. A holy card will be sufficient, along with an old set of keys. Peter (and Papa La-Bas) will appreciate the attention and will see to it that good luck flows into your house while misfortune is kept outside.

As anyone in New Orleans will tell you, it's to your best advantage to be on good terms with the gatekeeper. Keeping his image in your house will catch his attention, but he'll work even harder for you if you provide him with lagniappe ("something extra" in Louisiana French, by way of the American Spanish la ñapa, by way of the Quechua yapay). Papa La-Bas will appreciate a yellow or a white candle burned in his honor on Mondays, and he is also fond of candy or spare change left by your doorstep or at a nearby crossroads. The more attention you give him, the more assistance he will provide for you—and when the time comes, he may even usher you to the front of the line and past the velvet rope outside the heavenly gates.

Tales of Papa La-Bas

As a child young Antoine Domino learned how to play piano from his older brother, and by the age of fourteen he had dropped out of school and was playing in clubs throughout New Orleans. When he hooked up with bandleader Dave Bartholomew, he scored his first hit—and got a new stage name, "Fats" Domino — with the 1949 boogie-blues tune "The Fat Man." Looking for a follow-up, Domino and Bartholomew tapped into the legend of Papa La-Bas with 1950's "Hey! La Bas Boogie."

"Eh La Bas" was a Cajun jazz standard popular throughout New Orleans and was frequently sung at Mardi Gras. In 1886 George Washington Cable published a transcription of an early version of this in his The Dance in the Place Congo. Musicologists have noted the resemblance between this version and songs found in Guadeloupe, Martinique, Trinidad, and Santo Domingo. The original chorus spoke to the narrator's "chere cousin" and discussed the joys to be had in a Cajun kitchen. While this would seem to be an appropriate subject for the portly Domino, he and Bartholomew took the song in a different direction. Drawing upon the African "call and response" tradition, they turned "Eh! La Bas" ("Hey, Over There!") into a greeting, encouraging the audience to shout it back. Scholar Henry Louis Gates has suggested that "eh là-bas" was actually a coded reference to the pan-African god of the crossroads. Gates said:

Called Papa Legba as his Haitian honorific and invoked through the phrase "eh là-bas" in New Orleans jazz recordings of the 1920s and 1930s, Pa Pa La Bas is the Afro-American trickster figure from black sacred tradition. His surname, of course, is French for "down" or "over there," and his presence unites "over there" (Africa) with "right here." He is indeed the messenger of the gods, the divine Pan-African interpreter, pursuing, in the language of the text, "The Work," which is not only Vaudou but also the very work (and play) of art itself.

Papa La-Bas appears to have appreciated the shout-out. While "Hey! La Bas Boogie" didn't chart, other Domino and Bartholomew efforts like "Ain't That a Shame" and "Blueberry Hill" went on to become classics, making both men wealthy. Today both Domino and Bartholomew remain active. Bartholomew still occasionally plays trumpet at the Preservation Hall jazz club, which is appropriately located at 726 St. Peter Street. Domino has stayed put in New Orleans since the 1980s (with a brief relocation during Katrina), claiming he couldn't get a decent meal outside the city.

Yet another take on Papa La-Bas comes from noted black American writer Ishmael Reed. In Reed's 1972 book Mumbo Jumbo, a Harlem houngan named Papa La-Bas goes on a Pynchonesque journey in an effort to understand the new viral dance craze sweeping 1920s America, Jes Grew. Along the way he encounters resistance from members of the Wallflower Order and the Knights Templar, sinister secret societies dedicated to stamping out dancing and keeping the black man down. But he also finds aid from the old Hoodoo magician Black Herman and from his daughter Earline, an avatar of the Haitian lwa Erzulie. Reed's rollicking tale incorporates historical black figures like millionairess C. J. Walker, Claude McKay, and Countee Cullen, as well as Warren G. Harding (who was rumored to have black ancestry and who winds up at a Harlem rent party in this story). As befits a story featuring Papa La-Bas, it combines various narratives in a metafiction that both tells a story and comments on the process of storytelling and mythmaking.

While most African diaspora practitioners identify as Christians and incorporate Christian imagery and prayers into their spiritual practices, Mumbo Jumbo presents the Christian influence as an infiltration perpetrated by the Atonists, monotheists who have been working for world domination since the days of the Egyptian pharaoh Akhenaton. Instead of a servant of Bondye, the one true god (Papa's role in Haitian Vodou), Papa La-Bas becomes a major player in the war against his forces and a crusader for a polytheistic worldview that recognizes the importance of African tradition and that favors direct experience and practice over rote memorization and imitation. This is not surprising, given that Reed is also the author of the poem "Neo-Hoodoo Manifesto" and has stated, "Neo-HooDoo believes that every man is an artist, and every artist a priest."

Reed's take on Papa La-Bas may differ from others—but Papa has always defied easy description and reveled in ambiguity. And it seems that his Papa La- Bas resonated with many readers. Mumbo Jumbo, Reed's third novel, became his first major success and transformed him from a cult favorite into one of America's leading black writers and intellectuals. One might even say that the Old Man at the Crossroads had rewarded Reed and Domino for their devotion— and with that we come to one of the South's most enduring legends.

The Old Man at the Crossroads

It is one of the most well known of blues clichés: the talented musician who goes to a nearby intersection to make a deal with the Devil. Robert Johnson supposedly gained his legendary guitar skills after selling his soul to Ol' Scratch, and others have said that Charlie Parker gained fame after making a midnight trip to the crossroads. At first glance this may seem merely a retelling of the famous Faust legend, but closer analysis reveals a direct connection to central and southern Africa.

In the Kongo many oaths are taken on a cross scratched on the ground. The horizontal line represents this world and its position between the land of the gods and the land of the deceased ancestors. The vertical line is a pathway across that boundary, marking the relationship between the gods, man, and the dead. The oathtaker stands upon the cross, taking a place between life and death; in taking the oath, the person invokes the judgment and witness of both God and the ancestors.6 (A similar tradition has survived in African American Hoodoo, in which many practitioners use powders to draw a circle with a cross inside, an X, or a "five-spot" dice pattern when working magic.) The crossroads, where two paths meet, is a real-world representation of this important cosmology. Much as a large stone may be recognized in India as a lingam, or representative of Shiva, a crossroads became a sacred place where the spirit world could be contacted by those brave enough or foolish enough to seek it out.

In the Mississippi River Delta and along the Gulf Coast they claimed the crossroads was the home of "the Old Man," or "the Devil." While it is tempting to dismiss this identification as Christian brainwashing, it too has roots in African traditions. Along with great power the crossroads harbored danger. Bandits and highway robbers often lurked near the intersection, waiting for unwary travelers. A wrong turn might send you deep into the wilderness or unfriendly territory. Other cultures have noted a sinister side to the crossroads. In the Hellenic world, Hecate, patroness of sorcery, was saluted at the crossroads along with Hermes, the messenger. In Europe suicides and executed criminals were buried at the crossroads so their intranquil spirits would be unable to find their way back to haunt their neighbors and loved ones. The identification of the Old Man at the

Crossroads with the Christian Devil may not be entirely accurate, but neither is it completely unjustified.

That being said, the Old Man at the Crossroads appears to have little interest in acquiring souls. And while some claim he brings his devotees easy money and fame, those who know better realize that he actually teaches marketable skills. Bluesman Tommy Johnson (whom many believe provided the prototype for the more famous story about Robert Johnson) described the ritual as he performed it.

If you want to learn how to make songs yourself, you take your guitar and you go to where the road crosses that way, where a crossroads is. Get there, be sure to get there just a little 'fore 12 that night so you know you'll be there. You have your guitar and be playing a piece there by yourself. . . .

A big black man will walk up there and take your guitar and he'll tune it. And then he'll play a piece and hand it back to you. That's the way I learned to play anything I want.

Robert Johnson and Charlie Parker were not particularly promising musicians when they began their careers. Parker was laughed off the stage at Kansas City's High Hat when he first attempted jamming with a local band. Blues legend Son House, who knew Johnson, described Johnson's early attempts to play as "such a racket you never heard! It'd make the people mad, you know. They'd come out and say, 'Why don't y'all go in and get that guitar away from that boy! He's running people crazy with it!'" And while both became famous for their technical wizardry, it didn't happen overnight. Parker's playing improved dramatically after years of practicing as much as fifteen hours a day, while Johnson spent time training with blues artists like Son House and Ike Zinnerman. So while the Old Man at the Crossroads may have given them a lesson, they did plenty of homework beforehand and afterward.

If you wish to improve your skills, you can visit the Old Man at the Crossroads yourself. While there are varying accounts of how this is accomplished, most agree that you need to be at the crossroads at midnight: he prefers a liminal time and a liminal space. Some say that you need to visit for nine consecutive midnights; others declare that one visit will do. Bring your chosen instrument—your laptop, your guitar, your dice, or whatever else you use when practicing your chosen skill. You can bring an offering for the spirit if you want to further encourage him to come. A silver "Mercury" dime is appropriate (even though it actually bears an image of the Goddess Liberty wearing a winged cap, it has come to be associated with Hermes the Messenger by Hoodoo and New Orleans Voodoo practitioners). Others have brought black chickens or even offered their music as entertainment. Sit by the crossroads and practice your craft, and in time you will be visited by a black man. He may take your instrument from you, or take hold of your hands, or just whisper advice into your ear. If you can resist the urge to run away screaming, you'll find your abilities greatly improved when he leaves. Throw in some dedication and practice, and you may even find people commenting on your uncanny mastery of your craft. How far you take the Old Man's lessons is entirely up to you.

THE DIVINE MOTHER

The Virgin Mary

For the Anglophone Protestants who came to New Orleans after the Louisiana Purchase—and for many Protestants today—veneration of Mary was a form of idolatry and diabolism. They claimed Catholics were not honoring the Virgin Mother of God but rather worshipping the Whore of Babylon condemned in the Bible's Book of Revelation as "Mother of Harlots and Abominations of the Earth" (Revelation 17:5). This did not discourage the devout and not-so-devout of New Orleans from continuing to honor her as patroness of their beloved city.

Although they have become popular in the Crescent City since the 1970s, the Haitian lwa Ezili Freda and Ezili Dantor were not traditionally served in New Orleans Voodoo. Instead, those seeking the aid of the divine feminine put their trust in Mary. Christ is King of Heaven, and many of the male saints were knights, royals, and wealthy warriors. Mary was a poor peasant girl who was chosen for her humility, piety, and loving nature. The righteous relied on her power as Queen of Angels, while sinners pled for her forgiveness and understanding. And while God might refuse your petition, he was certain to take it more seriously if his mother asked him for a favor. Even if you have been put off by the excesses committed in the name of Christ and his church, you will find his mother to be a sympathetic, powerful, and loving protector and friend.

Mariology

In 431 the First Council of Ephesus referred to Mary as Theotokos, or God- bearer. A homily from St. Proclus shows the regard in which she was held by many of the early Church Fathers.

O man, run through all creation with your thought, and see if there exists anything comparable to or greater than the holy Virgin Mother of God. Circle the whole word, explore all the oceans, survey the air, question theskies, consider all the unseen powers, and see if there exists any similar wonder in the whole creation.

Even at this early date there was controversy about Mary's role in Christian theology. Nestorius and many of his followers declared that she was not Theotokos, but Christokos—bearer of Christ and mother of his human form but not his divine nature. While the Council of Ephesus, and the 451 Council of Chalcedon, declared Nestorius and his followers heretics, he continued to be influential in the East and is still considered a Church Father by Syrian Rite Christians.

As Christianity grew and became the dominant religion of the former Roman Empire, so too did devotion to Mary. Shrines in her honor appeared throughout Europe and the Byzantine world. Legends spread that Mary had been assumed body and spirit into heaven upon her death and that she had been conceived without sin so as to be a fitting vessel for the Savior. And if she was honored by the Church hierarchy, she was loved by the faithful, who showered her with adulation and praise.

Marian devotion was always particularly strong in France. As early as 185 St. Iraneus of Lyons had said, "The knot of Eve's disobedience was loosed by the obedience of Mary. For what the virgin Eve had bound fast through unbelief, this did the virgin

Mary set free through faith." The country's greatest cathedral was devoted to Notre Dame du Paris (Our Lady of Paris). And Bernard de Clairvaux (later, St. Bernard), who declaimed at length on Mary's role as Mediatrix between God and Man, admonished his followers:

In dangers, in doubts, in difficulties, think of Mary, call upon Mary. Let not her name depart from your lips, never suffer it to leave your heart. And that you may more surely obtain the assistance of her prayer, neglect not to walk in her footsteps. With her for guide, you shall never go astray; while invoking her, you shall never lose heart; so long as she is in your mind, you are safe from deception; while she holds your hand, you cannot fall; under her protection you have nothing to fear; if she walks before you, you shall not grow weary; if she shows you favor, you shall reach the goal.

Another movement that got its start in southern France and northern Italy was strongly devoted to the Virgin. The troubadours were enamored of the idea of courtly love—a chaste passion for a beautiful but inaccessible lover. Combining elements of Arab love poetry with Cathar imagery and popular music, troubadours traveled throughout France and Europe singing of the Virgin and inspiring others to follow their example. During their heyday (the eleventh through thirteenth centuries), Marian devotion reached a fever pitch.

But even after the troubadours faded from the scene, Mary remained an important part of religious life. Her statues were regularly decorated with flowers; while roses and lilies were particularly popular, other common offerings included violets (symbolizing Mary's modesty), marigold ("Mary's gold," offered in place of coins), snowdrops (for Mary's purity), and foxglove (also known as Our Lady's glove, or in France, le gant de Notre Dame). Paradise gardens, cloistered enclosed spaces filled with her favorite flowers, were dedicated to her in honor of her beauty and virginity.

As the Middle Ages gave way to the Renaissance, Marian art became increasingly popular. Franco-Flemish composer Josquin des Prez, one of the most influential musicians of fifteenth-and early sixteenth-century Europe, produced Marian tributes like Missa Ave Maris Stella, Missa de Beata Virgine, and Missa Mater Patris. Nicholas Poussin painted Holy Family on the Steps in 1648 and Assumption of Mary in 1650, and Jacques Stella painted The Nativity in 1639. (Perhaps he was hoping to win favor from Louis XIII, who at the urging of Cardinal Richelieu dedicated the French throne to the Virgin in 1638.)

With the Renaissance came the Reformation and a move away from Marian devotions. Later the Enlightenment treated veneration of Mary as just another silly superstition. Intellectuals and worldly folk began neglecting the Virgin. But the common people retained their great love for her even in the face of persecution during the French Revolution. This devotion was carried over to the French colonies, including their riverfront city in the New World.

Our Lady of Prompt Succor

Our Lady of Prompt Succor, you are most powerful against the enemy of our salvation. Through your Divine Son you crushed the serpent's head; hasten, then, to our help and deliver us from the deceits of Satan. Intercede for us with Jesus that we may always accept God's graces and be found faithful to Him. As you once saved New Orleans from ravaging flames and our Country from an invading army, have pity on us and obtain for us protection from hurricanes and all other disasters. Assist us in the many trials that beset our path through life. Be to us truly

In 1727 twelve Sisters of St. Ursula arrived in the then-primitive settlement of New Orleans after an arduous journey from France. Some were less than impressed with their new surroundings—one young nun wrote home that "upon seeing New Orleans for the first time, I can only say it looks like a large cesspool." But the sisters triumphed over adversity, establishing a convent and doing their best to preserve Catholic morals under adverse conditions.

But by 1803 the Ursuline Academy was facing a serious shortage of teachers and nuns. Mother André Madier wrote to France asking that more teachers be sent, but the bishop denied her request. The Church in France was under siege by the forces of the French Revolution, and he felt he had no nuns to spare. Mother André's only recourse was to appeal to Pope Pius VII, but that was a long shot indeed, since the Pope was a prisoner of Napoleon. Undeterred, her relative in France, Mother Saint Michel, sent a note to the Pontiff and petitioned the Virgin for aid, promising her, "O most Holy Virgin Mary, if you obtain for me a prompt and favorable answer to this letter, I promise to have you honored at New Orleans under the title of Our Lady of Prompt Succor."

The prayer was granted. Within two weeks after the letter was posted, the Pope sent more nuns to the Ursuline Academy. Mother Saint Michel commissioned a statue in honor of Our Lady of Prompt Succor, and on December 31, 1810, they placed the image of the Madonna holding the Infant Jesus in the academy's chapel.

Soon after, Our Lady helped the nuns yet again during the great fire of 1812. As the Vieux Carré burned, the winds began driving the fire toward Jackson Square and the Ursuline convent. As evacuation began, a nun named Sister St. Anthony placed a small statue of Our Lady of Prompt Succor on a window seat, and Mother St. Michel began to pray aloud, "Our Lady of Prompt Succor, we are lost unless you hasten to our aid!" As she prayed the wind shifted direction, blowing the flames back and allowing the fire to be extinguished. Amid the devastation the convent was one of the only buildings to be spared.

Three years later Our Lady of Prompt Succor came through for New Orleans yet again. On January 7, 1815, General Andrew Jackson and his six thousand troops were facing fifteen thousand British soldiers. All that night the nuns as well as many of the city's faithful gathered in the chapel in a prayer vigil, begging the Virgin for her aid. Mother Ste. Marie Olivier de Vezin, the convent's prioress, vowed that a Mass of Thanksgiving would be sung annually for Our Lady should the American forces win. On the morning of January 8, as the priest was offering communion, a messenger ran into the church and announced the British had been defeated.

General Jackson went to the convent himself to thank the nuns for their prayers: "By the blessing of heaven, directing the valor of the troops under my command, one of the most brilliant victories in the annals of war was obtained."

Today the Our Lady of Prompt Succor shrine is still located at the Ursuline Academy, now on 2635 State Street. During hurricane season the congregation requests her help at every Mass, and when a hurricane threatens, the faithful gather before her statue to recite the rosary and recite the prayer "Our Lady of Prompt Succor, hasten to help us!" After Katrina, congregants gathered to ask her assistance in ensuring aid from state and federal agencies and in rebuilding their devastated city.

The Holy Rosary

In 1203 a Spanish priest named Father Dominic Guzman was sent to the Languedoc region of southern France to confront the Cathar heresy. But he had little success; while the Catholic clergy was largely worldly and had little interest in the poor, the Cathar prefects were noted for their piety, sanctity, asceticism, and approachability. Dominic realized that he would win the souls of the Cathari commoners only by setting a good example and by feeding their hunger for knowledge and righteousness. As he said to Papal legates in a later rebuke. It is not the display of power and pomp, cavalcades of retainers, and richly-houseled palfreys, or by gorgeous apparel, that the heretics win proselytes; it is by zealous preaching, by apostolic humility, by austerity, by seeming, it is true, but by seeming holiness. Zeal must be met by zeal, humility by humility, false sanctity by real sanctity, preaching falsehood by preaching truth.

But despite his best efforts, he achieved little success in converting the people back to the True Faith. Then one day while he was in prayer, the Virgin appeared before him and said, "Wonder not that you have obtained so little fruit by your labors, you have spent them on barren soil, not yet watered with the dew of Divine grace. When God willed to renew the face of the earth, He began by sending down on it the fertilizing rain of the Angelic Salutation. Therefore preach my Psalter composed of 150 Angelic Salutations and 15 Our Fathers, and you will obtain an abundant harvest."

For most of the Catholic Church's history, the laity was unfamiliar with the clergy's complex rituals. Few could read and write in their native tongue, let alone the Latin used by monks and priests. They knew the biblical stories and possibly even a few scattered verses, but were unable to read the Scriptures or to recite the long chants of the Breviary. But they knew the simple prayers, especially the Ave Maria (Hail Mary) and the Paternoster (Our Father). So when they wished to petition God, Jesus, and the saints they would recite 50 or 150 Hail Marys, and to keep an accurate count of their Aves they used a knotted cord. Dominic encouraged this among the people and began making some headway against the heresy. Ultimately the Church decided a crusade would accomplish the task more quickly and wiped out the Cathars with armies instead of prayer—but the tradition of the Rosary remained and became an important tool for contemplation among Catholics in France and throughout the world.

To pray the Rosary, you begin by making the sign of the cross and say the Apostles' Creed.

I believe in God, the Father Almighty, Creator of Heaven and earth; and in Jesus Christ, His only Son Our Lord,

Who was conceived by the Holy Spirit, born of the Virgin Mary, suffered under Pontius Pilate, was crucified, died, and was buried.

He descended into Hell; the third day He rose again from the dead;

He ascended into Heaven, and sitteth at the right hand of God, the Father Almighty; from thence He shall come to judge the living and the dead.

I believe in the Holy Spirit, the holy Catholic Church, the communion of saints, the forgiveness of sins, the resurrection of the body and life everlasting. Amen.

After this you say one Our Father:

Our Father, who art in heaven Hallowed be thy name Thy Kingdom come, thy will be done on earth as it is in heaven

Give us this day our daily bread and forgive us our trespasses as we forgive those who trespass against us and lead us not into temptation but deliver us from evil. Amen.

Followed by one Hail Mary:

Hail Mary, full of grace, the Lord is with thee Blessed art thou amongst women and blessed is the fruit of thy womb Jesus Holy Mary, Mother of God Pray for us sinners Now and at the hour of our death. Amen.

Continue with one Glory Be:

Glory be to the Father, and the Son and the Holy Spirit as it was in the beginning, is now and ever shall be world without end. Amen.

You then announce the First Mystery and recite an Our Father. While meditating on that mystery, you say ten Hail Marys, followed by a Glory Be. Then you announce the Second Mystery, and repeat the process until all five mysteries are completed. The Mysteries are:

The Five Joyful Mysteries: The Annunciation of Gabriel to Mary that she was to conceive Jesus; Mary visits her cousin Elizabeth, who greets her with "Hail Mary, full of grace"; the birth of Jesus; the presentation of Jesus in the Temple; Jesus is found in the Temple preaching to the Rabbis.

The Five Sorrowful Mysteries: The agony of Jesus in the garden of Gethsameni; Jesus is scourged; Jesus is crowned with thorns; Jesus carries his cross; the crucifixion.

The Five Glorious Mysteries: The resurrection; Jesus ascends into heaven; the Holy Spirit descends at Pentecost; Mary is assumed body and soul into heaven; Mary is crowned Queen of Heaven and Earth.

The Five Luminous Mysteries: The baptism of Christ in the River Jordan; the wedding at Cana, where Jesus turns water into wine; the proclamation of the Kingdom of God; the transfiguration of Jesus; the Last Supper.

The Joyful Mysteries are said on Mondays, Saturdays, Sundays of Advent, and Sundays from Epiphany until Lent; the Sorrowful Mysteries are said on Mondays, Saturdays, Sundays of Advent, and Sundays from Epiphany until Lent; the Glorious Mysteries are said on Wednesdays and Sundays; and the Luminous Mysteries (a recent addition by Pope John Paul II) are said on Thursdays.

You can also say a novena, a series of nine Rosaries on nine separate days. At the beginning of each Rosary, you offer your petition or request. You then say the Rosary while meditating on the mystery appropriate for that day. When your prayer is answered, you say another nine Rosaries for nine more days, but instead of a petition, you begin with a prayer of thanksgiving to the Virgin Mary for her intercessions on your behalf.

All this Catholic prayer and imagery may seem out of place in a book about Voodoo. But New Orleans folk spirituality has been strongly influenced by Roman Catholicism. This has a great deal to do with the Crescent City's history and culture. But perhaps more important is the fact that the Virgin and the Saints respond to prayers and intercede on behalf of those who ask for their aid. New Orleans Voodoo has always been a practical tradition, and its followers will happily call on any spirit who will answer their petitions.

SERPENT

Li Grand Zombi

In Christian mythology, snakes are associated with Satan, thanks largely to the Garden of Eden legend. According to that story sin and death came into the world when Ol' Splitfoot, in the guise of a serpent, tempted Eve to partake of the forbidden fruit. Many icons of the Virgin Mary picture her standing atop a globe and stomping on the head of a snake (since her son Jesus conquered sin, death, and the Devil, who messed things up in the first place). Still other stories discuss the "flaming serpent" who tormented the Israelites during their sojourn in the desert and the proverbial ungrateful child who brings more pain than a serpent's tooth.

In Africa snakes were viewed differently. Serpent veneration was found throughout much of the continent. A 1705 report shows how one English crew who made land at the African port of Whydah learned this the hard way:

An English Captain having landed some of his men and part of his cargo, they found a snake in their house, which they immediately killed without the least scruple, and not doubting but they had done a good work, threw out the dead snake at their door, where being found by the Negroes in the morning, the English preventing the question who had done the fact, ascribed the honour to themselves; which so incensed the natives, that they furiously fell on the English, killed them all and burned their house and goods.

The Fon-speaking peoples of Dahomey honored the great serpent Ayida, who stretched across the sky as a rainbow by day and shimmered among the stars as the Milky Way by night. The

Tumbuka of central Malawi paid homage to the sky-dwelling python Chikangombe. The Bantu of central and southern Africa had Monyoha, the great water snake who ensured that the rivers and lakes would never dry up for those who honored him. And during the Middle Passage and the horrors of slavery, this snake veneration was carried to the New World, particularly New Orleans.

The Snake Dances of New Orleans

Writing in 1895, New Orleans journalist Henry C. Castellanos described a Voodoo ritual.

The King and Queen take their positions at one end of the room, near a species of altar, on which is placed a box, wherein the serpent is imprisoned, and where the affiliated can view it outside the bars. As soon as a strict inspection assures them that no intruder is within hearing or sight, the ceremony begins by the adoration of his Snakeship, by protestations of fidelity to his cult, and of submission to his behests. . . .

[The Voudou King] suddenly seizes the precious box, lays it upon the floor, and places the Queen upon the lid. No sooner has her foot touched the sacred receptacle than she becomes possessed, like a new Pythoness. Her frame quivers, her whole body is convulsed, and the oracle pronounces its edicts through her inspired lips. On some she bestows flattery and promises of success, at others she thunders forth bitter invectives. . . .

As soon as the oracle has answered every question propounded, a circle is formed and the serpent is put back upon the unholy fane. Then each one presents his offering, and places it in a hat impervious to prying curiosity.

Snakes became an integral part of Voodoo rituals in New Orleans and throughout the Mississippi River Delta. Numerous titillating reports described how the entrance of the serpent was prelude to wild orgies of drumming, sexual abandon, and race-mixing. An 1894 report in the New York Times described a Mobile, Alabama, ceremony in which

As the strokes of the tom-tom and the banjo quicken, a bacchanalian abandon takes the place of the usually decorous demeanor of the negro. A vigor unknown to polite society characterizes his steps and contortions of body. . . . The women tear off their clothing and re-enter the furious revel almost nude, shouting aloud with the rest of the company. . . . A naked white girl acted as a voodoo priestess wrought up to frenzy by dances and incantations that followed the sacrifice of a white and black hen. A serpent, trained to its part, and acted on by the music, coiled around the limbs of the girl, its motions studied by the votaries dancing around or standing to watch its contortions. The spectator fled at last in horror when the poor girl fell writhing in an epileptic fit.

In New Orleans some conjure folk and rootworkers kept one or more snakes around their house. This served to establish their credibility as powerful magicians. They might explain this by quoting Scripture, more specifically Mark 16:18, wherein it is said that those who believe shall "take up serpents." Or they might use their scaly pets for sinister effect. Since most of their neighbors were terrified of snakes, their nonchalance might be read as a sign that they had made a pact with evil. Like the black cats of European witch legends, their reptiles were seen by outsiders as familiar spirits masquerading in the guise of animals. This helped cement the rootworker's reputation as a powerful sorcerer who could work miracles for clients.

But there is evidence that a fair bit of this snake veneration, as has often been the case in New Orleans, was done for the benefit of a paying audience. The ritual nudity described in the Alabama ceremony (and frequently mentioned in other descriptions of New Orleans Voodoo) is not found in African or Afro- Caribbean religious practices. And the lurid descriptions of snake handling were often not taken directly from eyewitnesses but from second-hand or even third- hand sources. (The Castellanos account referenced above was plagiarized almost word for word from a 1797 account of a Saint-Domingue ceremony by French lawyer and historian Moreau de Saint-Méry!)

Haiti had a reputation as a savage place filled with witchcraft and Satanic rituals. Even a century later, the bloody tales of the uprising and the revenge of the slaves still resonated in a city where ruling whites tried to maintain control over the black population. The rumors of primitive Voodoo rituals in the bayous simultaneously terrified and titillated wealthy New Orleanians, especially when combined with accounts of overheated Negro sexuality in action. Since snake veneration was one of the most well-known and controversial aspects of Haitian spirituality, a serpent added that air of authenticity to a "religious ceremony" that was essentially a nudie show to the tourists.

This is not to say that snakes played no part in actual New Orleans Voodoo rituals. Marie Laveau, who was no stranger to the city's entertainment industry, drew upon the teachings and practices of Saint- Domingue and Africa for her work. In naming her famous snake "Li Grand Zombi," Laveau paid homage not to shambling animated corpses but to a powerful spirit—the Kongo creator Nzambi.

Nzambi, Simbi, and Li Grand Zombi

According to Kongo legend, Nzambi created the heavens, the earth, and the animals. Then, after creating man and woman, he taught them how to survive in his world and how to harness the magical power of his creation. By using those teachings they could break the blazing droughts and bring down the summer rain; they could heal sickness and ensure fertile crops. They could also communicate with the mpungas, deceased ancestors and nature spirits who assisted Nzambi in maintaining his creation. Today Nzambi is still honored in Cuba by practitioners of Las Reglas de Congo (also known as Palo Mayombe), who say "Nsambi primero," or "Nsambi is first."

Kongo cosmology envisioned the cosmos as two worlds—nza yayi (this world) and the nsi a bafwa (the land of spirits). Between these two worlds lay the kalunga, a vast ocean that served as threshold between the living and the dead. Because snakes were frequently seen climbing trees, burrowing beneath the ground, and resting in or near rivers or bodies of water, they were considered travelers between the realms. Since Kongo religious practices were concerned largely with commerce between the various worlds, it is not surprising that snakes play a major role in Kongo religions.

In Haiti, Vodouisants honor the Simbi family of lwa. Like the basimbi, snake spirits living in the rivers and streams of southern Africa, the Simbis are known to be shy but powerful magicians. Those who approach them with due patience and respect and gain their trust find they are powerful allies who can act as intermediaries between the worlds of flesh and spirit and life and death. Haitian houngan and author Milo Rigaud said of them:

The voodoo Mercury has the name of Simbi, a loa of many forms. He is the conductor of souls, who leads the souls of the dead in all directions bordered by the four magical orients of the cross. He is the Messiah of Legba, the messenger of the sun. Simbi corresponds to the hermetic Mercury of the cabalistic alchemy of the ritual sacrifice.

The lwa Simbi Makaya is one of the great sorcerers of Haitian Vodou. As patron of the secret Sanpwel society, he teaches his chosen followers powerful wangas (magical spells) that can be used for healing or destruction. Those who are not members regularly accuse the Sanpwel of human sacrifice, corpse desecration, and all sorts of related misdeeds. Within New Orleans, Li Grand Zombi had a similarly mixed reputation. Believers and practitioners considered the great serpent a benevolent protector and wise teacher. Those who were not so affiliated generally associated Grand Zombi with orgies and devil worship. As with Simbi Makaya, one's attitude toward Grand Zombi marked your status within the group.

In New Orleans the snake served simultaneously to advertise to one's clientele and to set them apart as outsiders. This is similar to Simbi's liminal position in Haiti. As a traveler between worlds, Simbi is tough to pin down. One of the most popular Simbis, Simbi Andezo, literally resides "in two waters" (an de zo), occupying the space where freshwater meets the salty ocean. Li Grand Zombi is similarly placed between public Voodoo rituals for tourists and private devotions, between religion and entertainment, between African roots and American money-making spectacles. In this, he is a fitting patron for the city of New Orleans and its religion.

The best way to honor Li Grand Zombi is with a live snake. This is not a commitment to be undertaken lightly. Taking responsibility for a pet is no small matter, especially when that pet is also a spirit animal! While snakes are relatively low-maintenance companions, they have certain needs that must be met. If not provided with appropriate temperatures and humidity, they are likely to become ill and die. A suitably large cage must be procured, along with a supply of the proper food.

A snake that is going to be handled in public ritual also needs to have a suitably tractable disposition—and when stressed, even the most docile snake may respond by biting, musking, or defecating on the nearest available target. That large python you are dancing with may be less impressive when you are soaked with runny snake dung or nursing a bloody open wound. Providing guidelines for the care of your personal Grand Zombi is beyond the scope of this book. As with any other pet, do your research before making your purchase, and make sure you are able to live up to your commitment.

Should you be unable to do so at this time, there is no shame in admitting this. Snake sheds can also be used as offerings for Grand Zombi, as well as snake statues or imagery. I do not recommend using snake skins, since they are harvested by killing the animals. (You want to honor the great serpent, not present him with the corpse of one of his siblings!) These can be placed on an altar along with offerings of eggs, candles, or if you are rhythmically talented, drumming. All these will show your devotion and help you to establish a link with Li Grand Zombi.

St. Michael the Archangel—or Mr. Daniel Blanc

Daniel Blanc, mighty against wickedness, defend us against the snares and schemes of the evil one and his minions. You who are sovereign over all the angelic hosts, you who command the powers and principalities and hate that impiety and evil should triumph, hear my prayer. Cast down my enemies from their high places and help us to be worthy to sit in the thrones of the righteous.

With the re-creation of New Orleans Voodoo, many began to identify Marie Laveau's snake with the great white serpent Damballah. This is incorrect. Li Grand Zombi's roots are in the Kongo and Bantu religions of central and southern Africa, not in the West African cultures that honor the rainbow serpent Da. This is not to say that Damballah is not served by the root doctors and Voodoo queens of New Orleans. He is, although not in a way one might expect. In Haiti Damballah is one of the leading spirits honored in public Vodou ceremonies, while Simbi is a patron of the secret societies. Their positions are reversed in New Orleans Voodoo: Li Grand Zombi plays a public role, while Damballah is served largely by insiders and is little known to those who are not of the faith.

St. Michael the Archangel has a worldwide reputation as a powerful defender against evil. According to Christian legend, it was he who gave Lucifer his heavenly eviction notice. His icons frequently show him trampling on a demonic figure with his shield in one hand and his fiery sword in the other. But in New Orleans there is a belief that he will work for you faster and more effectively if you address him by his real name: Mr. Daniel Blanc. (Others say his name is really Danny or Blanc Dani.)

While this may seem to be a rather silly superstition, those who are familiar with Haitian Vodou will recognize a common praise name for Damballah: Blan Dani, or White Dani. He did not come to New Orleans as a serpent—perhaps because Simbi/Grand Zombi had already filled that role—but as a warrior and ruler over the angelic armies.

Writing in 1904, journalist and author Helen Pitkin described a Voodoo ritual that called on Archangel Michael with this song:

Blanc Dani,

Dans tous pays blanc L'a commandé

Blanc Dani, dans tous pays blanc

L'a commandé (Blanc Dani,

In all white countries He has command

Blanc Dani, in all white countries He has command)

While Damballah is generally seen as a peaceful and even-tempered spirit, he can wreak a terrible vengeance on evildoers. Those who think snakes are slow have never seen one strike at a threat or a prey item. Damballah's great love of purity and righteousness is matched by his loathing for injustice. Those who find themselves facing powerful enemies can count on him for assistance, so long as they are in the right. One does not trouble Damballah with trivial matters or ask for his help in wrongdoing.

To call on Daniel Blanc, use an image or statue of St. Michael the Archangel. Like Damballah, he is served with clean white cloths and white candles, and like Damballah, he is a fastidious spirit who prefers being served in a tidy home. Put his shrine atop a high shelf or in an elevated place to honor his position in heaven alongside the Most High. Make him offerings of sweet white foods like coconut or rice pudding.

THE VOODOO QUEEN

Marie Laveau

She was a skilled Voodoo priestess who led a huge coven of worshippers and used her magical abilities to amass great wealth and power. She was a charlatan whose primary expertise was in the arts of blackmail, pandering, and showmanship. She was a symbol of feminine power and triumph over the forces of racism and sexism—or a con artist preying on the vulnerable. There are innumerable myths about Marie Laveau; her story has been reinterpreted by various sources to support their cause or sell their products. Finding the facts about her life is considerably more challenging. If we are to learn more about the Crescent City's most famous native, we will need to deconstruct the legends to get at the kernels of truth contained therein.

Today most images of Laveau are based on an 1835 painting by portraitist George Catlin. It depicts an attractive copper-skinned woman of color with penetrating eyes and an enigmatic expression. She wears a lacy shawl and a yellow and red plaid tignon (an elaborate headwrap worn by New Orleans women of color). A copy of the 1835 painting still hangs at the Cabildo, a historic building in New Orleans, and is labeled "Marie Laveau, legendary African American Voodoo Queen during the early nineteenth century." But when Louisiana Writers' Project interviewers asked elderly blacks who remembered Laveau if the image resembled her, they all said it did not. Some of those interviewed said that Laveau was a dark-skinned black woman; others said she could have passed for white.

Although we cannot be sure what Marie Laveau looked like, the interviewees were unanimous in saying that she was a tall, strikingly beautiful woman with a magnetic presence and a regal manner befitting her later title as "Voodoo Queen of New Orleans." And the mystery that surrounds her appearance is matched only by the uncertainty surrounding many of the particulars of her life.

Birth and First Marriage

Some stories claim that Marie Laveau was born in Saint-Domingue; others say that she was the daughter of a white plantation owner and a slave. But according to a baptismal record in St. Louis Cathedral, Père Antonio de Sedella (better known as Père Antoine) baptized a six-day-old Marie Laveau on September 16, 1801. Her mother, Marguerite d'Arcantel, was a freed mulatto slave. Her father, Charles Laveau, was a prosperous free man of color who had made his fortune as a real estate speculator, money lender, and slave trader. She grew up in her grandmother's modest cottage on St. Ann Street, in the Creole neighborhood of Faubourg Tremé (in English, the Tremé suburb).

On August 4, 1819, Marie married a quadroon carpenter from Saint- Domingue named Jacques Paris. As a Saint-Domingue refugee, Paris would have been much sought after for his woodworking and construction skills. Saint- Domingue gens du couleur (people of color) were generally better trained and more skillful than those from still-rustic New Orleans. The newly married couple settled into what promised to be a comfortable but unexceptional middle-class life in a house on the 1900 block of North Rampart Street in another Creole neighborhood, Faubourg Marigny.

But tragedy soon struck, and Jacques Paris disappeared from the lives of Laveau and their two children. Perhaps he died in one of the yellow fever epidemics that regularly descended on New Orleans during the humid summers. Perhaps he deserted his wife and returned to the Free Black Republic of Haiti to seek his fortune. Perhaps, some would whisper darkly after Laveau became famous, he had been sacrificed to the African devils his wife served. Whatever the reason for his disappearance, by 1825 Laveau was calling herself the "Widow Paris," and a death certificate was filed with the authorities.

In his nonfiction book Voodoo in New Orleans and his novel The Voodoo Queen, Robert Tallant claimed that Laveau supported herself after Paris's disappearance by working as a hairdresser. Although evidence for this claim is murky, it is not unreasonable. At that time many New Orleans femmes du couleur (women of color) supported themselves by styling the locks of the city's wealthy and well-dressed white and mulatto women. Before one of the Crescent City's many social functions, women would hire a hairdresser to make sure their tresses were as lovely as their fine outfits. Hairdressing required both skill and artistic sense: a good stylist would work to emphasize the client's strongest features while drawing attention away from her weak points. She might take special pains to minimize any sign of kinky hair in a woman from a supposedly "white" family and dye any traces of gray for a belle whose youth was beginning to fade.

As a hairdresser, Laveau could certainly have gained the confidence of her clients and learned their secrets. She also may have provided them with Voodoo remedies, potions, and charms to win back a straying lover or attract a new one. But it seems that Laveau's tenure as a hairdresser was a relatively brief one. While one woman said that she "called herself a hairdresser, and that's how she got in the good graces of the fine people," another said she was "some kind of a hairdresser and seamster, but she did all that in her early days. Shucks, she soon cut that stuff out." It could be that she was beginning to focus on her trade in Voodoo, or it could be that she preferred to concentrate on the new man who had come into her life.

Christophe Glapion

In 1820s New Orleans, young white men frequently took free women of color as mistresses, set them up in houses, and fathered children with them, a practice known as plaçage. The women of these relationships were called placées. In 1840 femmes du couleur libre (free women of color) owned about 40 percent of the property in the Faubourgs Marigny and Tremé. Many of these homes were provided by white lovers who wanted to ensure the security of their placées. Often they would build a double Creole cottage, ensuring a home for their families and a steady means of support from rents paid on the other side. (Alternately, the second side could be used as a vacation home for the visiting man when he wished to spend time with his Creole lover.)

The only thing that made Christophe Glapion's arrangement with Marie Laveau unusual was her relatively advanced age (twenty-five) and her status as a widow who had already born children. Even for one of the young beauties who debuted at the city's quadroon balls, Glapion would have been a fine catch. Scion of an aristocratic French family with roots in Normandy, he had also served with distinction in the Battle of New Orleans. It is a tribute to Laveau's charisma and beauty that she was able to capture his heart. While many white New Orleanian men abandoned their placées after marrying a white bride, Glapion stayed with Laveau until his death in 1855.

Glapion's devotion to Laveau has inspired a number of legends. Some claimed that he was actually a free man of color, while others said that he had chosen to present himself as such so that he could live freely with Laveau and their two daughters. While some reports claim that Laveau bore fifteen children with Glapion, records indicate they had seven children, only two of whom survived to adulthood. Infant mortality in New Orleans was very high in those days. Laveau's two children by Paris both died young of yellow fever or one of the other epidemic diseases that frequently swept the city during the hot summers. Even his contemporaries were sometimes confused by his unseemly devotion to his colored mistress. An 1850 census listed all of the occupants of Laveau's home on 911 St. Ann Street, including the white Glapion, as "mulatto."

But while Glapion was a devoted husband, father, and grandfather, he was no great businessman. At the time of his death in 1855, he was heavily in debt, having mortgaged the family house and other properties in a desperate attempt to raise cash. The Citizens Bank of Louisiana foreclosed on the property and auctioned it off at a sheriff's sale on July 17, 1855. (Pierre Crocker, a prosperous free man of color and father of several of Laveau's grandchildren, purchased the house for $1,880 and gave the Laveau family a life estate on the premises.) Marie was now fifty-four years old, her longtime companion was dead, and she had few prospects for continued income. To support herself, she threw herself into the trade that would make her famous.

The Voodoo Queen

On July 2, 1850, Marie Laveau and another free woman of color, Rosine Dominique, filed a complaint before Recorder John Seuzenau seeking the return of a statue that had been confiscated during a June 27 raid on an illegal Voodoo gathering. The statue, described by a contemporary newspaper as "a quaintly carved figure resembling something between a centaur and an Egyptian mummy," was valued by Laveau at fifty dollars. Ultimately the court decided that it would be returned upon payment of $8.50 in court costs; the records show, however, that the fine was paid and statue taken not by Laveau but by an unknown "young quadroon."

This is the first mention of Laveau in connection with Voodoo. The priestess who presided over the gathering in question was a woman named Betsy Tolenado, who later charged the police with illegally breaking up a religious ceremony. (The court found that the arrest was valid, since it involved a gathering of mixed free people and slaves—a serious concern in those days of militant abolitionism.) But it seems she was already a personage of some importance in the Voodoo community, since she was willing to present herself before the court and claim ownership of some of the paraphernalia used at the ceremony.

In the summer of 1859 Marie Laveau's name appeared in the local newspapers. The Crescent unflatteringly referred to her as "the notorious hag who reigns over the ignorant and superstitious as the Queen of the Voodoos." They went on to report that her neighbor had complained that Laveau and her followers were "disturbing his peace and that of the neighborhood with their fighting and obscenity and infernal signing and yelling" during their "hellish observance of the mysterious rites of Voudou." No record exists as to the disposition of this complaint. It could be that Laveau used her Voodoo skills to woo the judge, or she may have made out-of-court arrangements with her neighbor to keep the noise down after dark. What we can surmise from these reports is that she was by this time holding ceremonies in her home and was recognized (by some journalists, at least) as a Voodoo Queen.

Around this time Laveau began officiating at the weekly public dances at Congo Square. These events, where blacks gathered together to perform African- inspired dances and drumming, were popular with citizens throughout the city's various racial and social strata. Laveau used these events to sell charms and services to observers, including wealthy white patrons. (She may have been inspired by Doctor John, who had become rich through catering to a white clientele.) Those who showed special interest might be allowed to attend services in Laveau's home, which was filled with statues, candles, and images of various saints. Or they might be invited to the annual St. John's Eve (June 23) ceremonies at Lake Pontchartrain. Once semisecret gatherings of devoted Voodoo practitioners, during Laveau's era they became far more popular with the "smart set." (Those who did not receive invites would frequently wander through the woods in search of the ceremony, but only rarely found it.)

In her later years Laveau became increasingly frail and was unable to attend many public functions. By 1869 Malvina Latour had taken her place as presiding officer at the St. John's Eve ceremonies. Laveau remained a figure of legend and terror in her neighborhood, with children running from the once-beautiful woman who now resembled classic portrayals of the "wicked witch." In the summer of 1881 Marie Laveau died. Writer Lafcadio Hearn penned a glowing eulogy for her. Although he had little sympathy for Voodoo, referring to it as "impious ceremonies of worshipping the prince of evil," he called Laveau "one of the kindest women who ever lived" and suggested she had been called a Voodoo Queen only because of her skill in herbal medicines.

Later, rumors would spread that Marie Laveau's daughter had taken her mother's place as Voodoo Queen. Robert Tallant and other writers would speak of "Marie Laveau I" and "Marie Laveau II." There is no evidence to suggest that any of Laveau's daughters followed in their mother's footsteps. It is possible that Tallant took the claims of interviewees who were too young to have known Laveau as evidence that her daughter continued the family trade, rather than proof his subjects were fabricating their stories. It is also possible that other rootworkers and Hoodoo women used Laveau's name or spread the rumor that they were related to her.

But whatever the case, Laveau's death did not end her fame or her notoriety. Her relative poverty at the time of her death was explained by claims that she had given away all her money to the poor. Legends and half-truths were repeated as facts, then repeated again. A widow who supported her extended family through Voodoo became one of the wealthiest and most feared citizens of New Orleans and founder of a dynasty that lasted through generations. And her grave became a site where many pilgrims came to offer their respects and to seek her otherworldly assistance.

The Tomb of Marie Laveau(s)

Perhaps the most famous grave in New Orleans is the Glapion Family Crypt in St. Louis Cemetery No. 1. One inscription on the tomb reads, "Marie Philome Glapion, décdé le 1 Juin 1897, ágée de Soixante-deux ans" ("Marie Philome Glapion, deceased June 11, 1897, aged sixty-two years"). Another inscription on the tomb reads, "Famille Vve. Paris / née Laveau" (Family of the Widow Paris, born Laveau), while a bronze tablet announces, under the heading "Marie Laveau," that "This Greek Revival Tomb Is Reputed Burial Place of This Notorious 'Voodoo Queen.'"

Some have claimed that Marie Laveau was buried elsewhere, as was her daughter. Several other tombs have been credited as the resting place of each. But Laveau I's 1881 obituary claimed that she had been buried in her family tomb in St. Louis Cemetery No. 1, and most believers consider the Glapion crypt to be where both Laveaus are interred. As a result, it has gained widespread attention from the curious, the lovelorn, and the tourists seeking an "authentic"

New Orleans Voodoo experience.

Visitors seeking the favor of the Voodoo queen have long left small gifts at her tomb. Coins, Mardi Gras beads, flowers, rum, and candles are often left at the site. Robert Tallant described the rituals that took place at the "Marie Laveau tomb" at St. Louis Cemetery No. 2:

Its slab is always covered with literally hundreds of crosses made with red brick. Until recently there was a crack in the slab, and into this devotees would drop coins and make a wish. There was a particular belief here that any girl wishing a husband could be certain of having her desire fulfilled. The rite consists of rapping on the slab three times, saying the wish out loud, then making a cross with red brick, a piece of which always reposes on top of the row of crypts. This place is also known as the "Wishing Vault" and the "Voodoo Vault," and probably more Voodoos will accept it as the burial place of Marie Laveau than they will the tomb in St. Louis Cemetery No. 1.

However, others will tell you that this is a mistake, and that another Voodoo queen, Marie Comtesse, is buried here, that in some way the two became confused. The sexton will tell you that "there ain't nothing in that oven but some old bones of people what died of Yellow Fever. I don't know how this started, but they keep coming—white and colored—and making their crosses. It's a damned nuisance."

Today it has become customary to draw three Xs on the tomb while making a wish. This is generally done using a piece of crumbling brick, although some use charcoal and others use permanent markers or other graffiti tools. Along with the inevitable Xs, the Glapion tomb is now decorated with hearts, pentagrams, poetry, and initials. Sextons regularly clean the crypt, but to no avail: the Laveau legend has ensured that as fast as old markings are removed, new ones take their place.

But while popular, this tradition is scorned by Voodoo practitioners as destructive and disrespectful. Many of the people making these brick Xs use chunks of brick they have pulled from other tombs, and many of the monuments around the Glapion crypt have sustained considerable damage from the demands of well-meaning wishmakers. One professional guide has claimed that the tradition of drawing Xs at St. Louis Cemetery No. 1 began with an early cemetery guide who wished to explain away some graffiti on the tomb. Thinking quickly, he described a "Voodoo custom," which then became part of the ever- growing Marie Laveau legend.

There is a long tradition that those who desecrate a gravesite can incur the wrath of the deceased spirit. Many New Orleans locals say that those who anger Marie Laveau will be haunted by the ghost of Li Grand Zombi, who was buried with her and who still protects his beloved mistress. Grand Zombi's zombie has been described as a massive coal-black snake who slithers between the tombs. Irreverent tourists who disrespected Laveau's tomb have reportedly awakened to find Grand Zombi beside them. Others have reported seeing a massive black cat with fiery eyes, or even the ghost of Marie Laveau herself, wandering through the cemetery in her finery and trademark red turban and muttering curses at evildoers. And if that isn't enough to keep you away from the nearby bricks, you may want to avoid the New Orleans police department. Marking graves or otherwise desecrating cemeteries can land you a stiff fine or a stay in one of the city's infamous jails. Don't take the chance. This is one tradition that deserves a decent burial.

THE WARRIORS

Joe Féraille, St. Marron, and Yon Sue

Throughout its long history, New Orleans has seen more than its share of violence. It's not surprising, then, that a number of warrior spirits are honored in New Orleans Voodoo. These hard-boiled fighters can assist you when you need a helping hand—but like all soldiers, they should be approached with caution. It's good to have them on your side—but it's even better not to have them working against you!

Joe Féraille

Laughing soldier, wily enemy, I call on your aid, Joe Féraille. Lend your strength to my cause and give me the courage I need to triumph. Do not lead me into danger, and do not tempt me into folly. Give me your cunning but not your madness. Let me stand firm as your anvil against the blows of my enemies and let your blade cut through the bonds that entangle me.

In West Africa the mighty spirit Gu was honored as the patron of blacksmiths, metalworkers, and soldiers. The Yoruba peoples honored him as Ogun, a mighty warrior, while the Fon of Dahomey placed him third in their pantheon, behind only the creators Mawu and Lisa. All considered him a great intercessor who could hack through all barriers and push aside any obstacle. During the dark days of the Middle Passage, he came to the New World, where he is still honored today. In Cuba people pay tribute to him as Ogun, master of iron, Brazilians honor him as Ogum, while Haitians call him Ogou. And in New Orleans he has become a well-known part of local folklore as "Iron Joe" or "Joe Féraille."

Haitian Vodou has many Ogous: Ogou Badagris is a cagey neg politik ("political guy" or diplomat), while Ogou Balindjo is a naval captain who answers to the ocean emperor Met Agwe, and Ogou San Jak is a cavalry knight represented by images of Saint James the Greater (in French, St. Jacques Majeur) on horseback. But while Ogou Feray is a general known for his short temper but also his loyalty to his family, Joe Féraille is a freebooter and smuggler. He may fight for your interests or your opponent's interests—but you can always be sure he is fighting for his own.

One traditional Cajun song (recorded by Edier Segura in 1934) tells the story of Joe Féraille trading his wife for a bucket of pecans. The pecan salesman may have thought he got the best of the bargain—until Mrs. Féraille ran away and returned to her husband! As the song goes on, Féraille acquires barrels of corn, peanuts, and other prizes in exchange for his lady. Each time he comes out of the trade wealthier than before, while the seller is left with nothing.

As is often the case with folk songs, one can find multiple layers of meaning behind the deceptively simple lyrics. Is Joe Féraille a populist hero who uses his wits to get the better of more prosperous businessmen? Is he a pimp making a tidy living with the aid of his woman? Is he a con artist taking advantage of hard-working farmers? However you may interpret Joe's actions, one thing is clear: if you trust him too much, you may find yourself poorer for your gullibility. Those who would work with Joe Féraille are advised to take that lesson to heart.

A darker take on Joe comes from contemporary Cajun singer Zachary Richard. His "Joe Férraille" begins with the narrator in prison. As he awaits execution he sings to his mother, who awaits outside the gates, and to the girl who loved him but who has forgotten him. He also lays special blame on Joe, that "goddamn canaille" (rabble, blackguard) who sold him whiskey, then loaned him a pistol. The sad tale ends with the narrator awaiting the dawn, when he will be dancing on the gallows.

Richard captures an important truth about Iron Joe and about the various faces of Gu. He is an ambivalent figure who can get you in a great deal of trouble if you aren't careful. Yoruba legends tell of Ogou swimming in rivers of blood and slaying friend and foe alike when he flies into a berserk rage. Joe Féraille will happily sell you his whiskey, then loan you his weapons when you're in a fighting mood. But once you sober up, you may find yourself paying a terrible price for your actions. When you go drinking with Joe, you had best be sure you can hold your liquor.

If you wish to work with Joe Féraille, you may do best to treat him as a mercenary for hire. If he respects you, he will do his best to honor your requests—provided, of course, that you pay him a fitting salary for his efforts. As with any mercenary, you will need to keep an eye on him and make sure that you are getting your money's worth. A small payment beforehand with the promise of a larger one after you see results is a good approach. Make absolutely sure that you carry through with your end of the bargain if Joe carries through with his, and you'll find that he is a quick and powerful worker.

You can serve Joe with red candles and booze; like all his African and Caribbean brothers, Joe is a prodigious drinker. An image of a pirate or a mercenary soldier can be used to represent him. A cutlass or scimitar would be a worthy offering, as would bullets or a pistol. (But be sure to take appropriate gun safety precautions if you do. Remember that Joe doesn't mind lending out his weapon to people who might not be in a state of mind to use it!) And always be on your guard when you're dealing with him. Like many New Orleans locals, Joe isn't afraid of taking advantage of those who are naïve or careless.

St. Marron

Oh, St. Marron, I seek your aid in my hour of need. As you were able to break your chains and find your freedom, help me to avoid the snares of those who would capture me. In my hour of darkness and fear I call upon you. Pray for me that I may go about my business untroubled and that my enemies may be caught up in their own pitfalls.

Those slaves who escaped from captivity often made their way to the cypress swamps. There they established colonies of maroons (from the Spanish cimarrón, or fugitive) or, in French, marrons. Joining forces with other escaped slaves and indentured servants, outlaws, pirates, and Indians fleeing colonial genocide, they created tight-knit communities protected by their inaccessibility.

Some sought a settled existence in which they could build farms and raise their families in freedom. Others supported themselves by raids on outlying farms. Maneuvering through the canebrakes and sloughs of the wild regions between plantations and towns, they established trade and smuggling networks with slaves and free persons of color. Scorned by the white establishment as savages and criminals, many became folk heroes to the black population.

The most famous of these marron bandits was an escaped slave named Squier. Squier was one of Congo Square's most brilliant dancers, known especially for his performance of the bamboula. His master, General William de Buys, had given him a gun and encouraged him to hunt on his own. Squier became not only a talented hunter but an expert marksman who taught himself how to shoot with both hands because of a premonition that he might one day lose his arm.

Squier's time in the wilderness gave him a taste of freedom. He tried to escape several times but each time was caught by slave hunters and returned to de Buys. In 1834 he was shot by patrollers; his injured right arm became infected and was ultimately amputated. As soon as his wound healed, Squier made yet another escape. This time he was able to make it to the swamps, where he joined a marron community and became infamous as the bandit Bras Coupé (Cut Arm).

For several years Bras Coupé and his marrons led a campaign of robbery and pillage against the settlers. The whites considered him the most dangerous bandit in the Louisiana swamps, spreading tales of his atrocities in whispers and offering ever-increasing rewards for his capture. But the slaves and free blacks told very different stories. Among them, Bras Coupé's exploits became legendary. Some claimed that he had superhuman powers and that he was immune to fire and bullets.

On July 18, 1837, Bras Coupé's luck ran out when he was killed by a Spanish fisherman named Francisco Garcia. Garcia claimed that he had been attacked while at work on his boat. Garcia grabbed an iron bar and beat the escaped slave to death in self-defense. (Skeptics suggested that Garcia was actually one of Coupé's henchmen and murdered him in his sleep for the bounty.) Whatever the circumstances of Bras Coupé's demise, his body was brought back to New Orleans, where it was displayed in Jackson Square as a warning to any other slave who might wish to escape bondage.

But though Bras Coupé was dead, he was still honored by many blacks as St. Marron. The stories of Squier's exploits were now told about this legendary escapee who led many other slaves to freedom and who avenged the wrongs committed against his people. In the best tradition of folk Catholicism and ancestor veneration, he became in death an honored protector of those who labored under the yoke of oppression and racism.

Even after slavery ended, black people in Louisiana still had plenty to fear from the wealthy and powerful whites. Where once they had enforced their will with slave hunters and overseers, they now used the police force to make sure black people "knew their place"—which was, of course, beneath respectable white citizens. Efforts to better one's lot through numbers-running, moonshine- distilling, or other profitable but illegal means were often met with beatings, arrests, and long sentences in Louisiana's notorious prisons. St. Marron was now called on to avoid confrontations with the police or to secure freedom for prisoners.

In death as in life, St. Marron is a secretive fellow. Those who work with him in New Orleans are generally loath to provide specific details of how he is served. Suitable offerings might consist of cornmeal, okra, and corned beef or other salted or cured meats—all foods that a marron might have eaten in the swamps. His shrine might include broken chains (to symbolize his escape from slavery) and an image of an escaped slave. You might burn a red candle to petition him. But ultimately you will have to go out into the wild and make contact with St. Marron yourself. He will let you know what he wants from you. Keep in mind that he may want to be left alone.

Yon Sue

Yon Sue, mighty warrior and king, hear my plea. Always you have been the champion of your people. You raise up the weak and bring low the mighty. King Agassou, panther who stalks in the night, strike down those who would do evil against me. As you led your people to their promised land, guide me through the darkness and protect me from the schemes of those who would hold me back.

Since the days of Marie Laveau, many in New Orleans have petitioned Saint Anthony of Padua by another name. When addressed as "Yon Sue," the benevolent old monk could become a powerful guardian. Indeed, some said that he was the special protector of those who followed the old African traditions. A few of his wealthy Creole followers claimed he was actually a mighty king. They wore red neckerchiefs in honor of their royal patron, whom they addressed as "Monsieur Agassou."

A bit of research will soon verify M. Agassou's regal bona fides. According to an African legend, a young princess named Aligbonon of Tado met a leopard in the jungle and fell in love with it. Their union produced a son named Agassou. When the king of Tado died, Agassou tried to ascend the throne. Alas, his claim was denied; while his mother's royal lineage was not in question, no one could determine whether his feline father was of the right social set.

Undeterred, Agassou and his followers left the kingdom and moved to the Abomey plateau (in modern-day Benin). There he proved his leadership credentials by setting up and ruling a small colony. The chief of one small nearby village, Da, complained that these new migrants were taking up so much room that they would soon be building a palace on his belly. Agassou responded by taking up arms against Da's village. After killing him, they threw him into a pit and proceeded to place their new palace atop his body. Its name, Dahomey, can be translated as "On the Belly of Da." To honor his divine ancestor, the new king chose the leopard as the heraldic symbol of his dynasty.

While skeptics may question tales of Agassou's divine parentage, none can dispute the success of his kingdom. Dahomey became famous for the discipline of its armies, including thousands of female soldiers, who were known to European observers as the Amazons of Dahomey. This military might allowed them to expand throughout the Abomey plateau and on toward the coast. In 1645 King Houegbadja declared that each Dahomean king should leave his successor more land than he inherited. His successors took his suggestion to heart, and by 1724 Dahomey had conquered the important port of Allada and had become an important slave-trading kingdom.

The slave trade brought great wealth to Dahomey's monarchy and to the artisans and weavers who worked to decorate its palaces and temples. But although Dahomey was flush with gold, it lacked in basic human freedoms. Each citizen of Dahomey owed absolute allegiance to the king, who was honored as Dada (father of the whole community), Dokounnon (holder and distributor of wealth), Sèmèdo (master of the world), and Aïnon (master of the earth), among other titles. The slightest disobedience could be punished by death. A court official who fell into royal disfavor, or a relative who might pose a challenge to the throne, could be sold into slavery.

But even in the New World those slaves who carried Agassou's blood continued to pay tribute to their half-divine ancestor. In New Orleans Yon Sue was known as the guardian of the old ways, the one who kept trouble away from the Voodoo queens and ensured they could continue their devotions to the African spirits. When the chips were down and legal or social pressures threatened the community, Yon Sue would make sure that his people survived to perform the traditional rituals. Police, crusading evangelists, and muckraking journalists regularly launched crusades against Voodoo and its believers, but Yon Sue saw to it that all their efforts came to naught.

To serve Yon Sue, you can get a small statue of Saint Anthony of Padua or a leopard or spotted panther figurine. Tie a red ribbon about the statue; as you do, welcome Yon Sue into his new home and offer him your respects. You can serve him with red candles, rare steak, and high-proof alcohol. Yon Sue is not one to be petitioned lightly: you don't trouble the king for trivial matters. But if you approach him with the appropriate reverence and respect, he will help you to triumph and prosper in the face of adversity.

If you are being harassed for your interest in Voodoo, you can ask Yon Sue for his aid—but make sure you are prepared for his response! Your tormentors may very well wind up dead or horribly injured. As a Dahomean king, Yon Sue has little patience for blasphemy and disrespect; he also knows the value of fear in maintaining order and discouraging wrongdoers. You may do better to call on him for advice in leading your group, or ask him to bless your rituals so that the spirits look upon them with favor.

THE MIRACLE WORKERS

St. Expidité, St. Jude, and St. Roch

When you're poor and disenfranchised, you need quick and powerful protectors. Many New Orleans natives know that all too well. In the ragged crime-ridden neighborhoods outside the tourist sections, lots of people are in need of miracles. While many saints and spirits will help out, some are known for being especially prompt and powerful. These miracle workers have become particularly popular in the Big Easy. If you are in need, you will find they are ready to lend you a hand.

St. Expedité

Oh, St. Expeditus, in you I place my hope that my petitions may be granted if they are for my own good. Please ask our Lord through the intercession of the Blessed Virgin for the forgiveness of my sins and the grace to change my life particularly (here mention the particular grace desired), and I promise to follow your examples and will propagate your devotion. Amen.

It has become one of the most popular fables of New Orleans folk Catholicism. The chapel of St. Anthony of Padua (a "mortuary chapel" built to perform funeral masses for victims of the city's frequent yellow fever epidemics) received several saint statues. One of the boxes lacked a label identifying the saint whose statue appeared therein. It did, however, have an Expedité (rush shipping) sticker attached. The uneducated New Orleans locals assumed this was the saint's name and began making prayers to "Saint Expedité." As befits his name, St. Expedité soon acquired a reputation for performing quick and frequent miracles. Before long he was one of New Orleans' most popular and frequently propitiated saints.

The story, while amusing, is an urban legend that has several variants. According to the original version, a packing case containing a martyr's relics was sent to a community of Parisian nuns in or around 1798. The nuns allegedly misread the Expedité sticker and began asking St. Expedité to intervene on their behalf. When he did, his veneration spread rapidly throughout France and other Catholic countries. And Reunion, a French-speaking island in the Indian Ocean near Mauritius, claims St. Expedit as their patron. According to their story, the colonials requested religious relics from the Vatican and received a box labeled Expedit (dispatched). Historical evidence suggests that the cult of St. Expedité began in seventeenth-century Italy and spread to Germany. In 1781 the Sicilian town of Acirale declared Expeditus their patron saint.

Once we get past the legends, we know very little about the original St. Expeditus. He was apparently a Roman centurion stationed in Armenia, one of the early strongholds of Christianity. When he decided to become a Christian, the Devil sent a crow to tempt him with its cries of "Cras! Cras!"—Latin for "Tomorrow! Tomorrow!" But Saint Expeditus was not to be deterred. He grabbed the crow, threw it to the ground, and stomped on it, declaring, "I shall become a Christian today!" Later he achieved the crown of martyrdom when he was killed during Emperor Diocletian's Great Persecution of 303.

Expeditus is typically shown as a young Roman centurion. In his hands he holds a cross inscribed with the Latin word hodie, meaning "today." Beneath his foot is a dying crow, which is sometimes declaring "cras, cras" with its dying breath. As a result, he is frequently called upon to discourage procrastination or in situations where quick action is required. He has also gained a following among computer programmers and hackers. As Kathy Dupon, a freelance computer consultant living in New Orleans, says,

I'm not a big believer in the saints, but St. Expedité is another whole story—he's so good he's scary. My clients were forever paying me late until I taped a card with the saint's picture behind my mailbox as a joke last year. Now my checks almost always arrive on time.

St. Expedité is most commonly served with red candles and a glass of water on his left-hand side. After he intercedes on your behalf, you should give him a gift of flowers and a slice of pound cake as a reward. (If you do not give him his due, it is said that he will take back everything he has done on your behalf.) You should also let others know about his assistance. In New Orleans his name frequently appears in classified ads as grateful patrons offer their public thanks for his private favors.

Should you develop a personal relationship with St. Expedité, you may consider setting up an altar on his behalf. His statues, images, holy cards, and candles are readily available in most botanicas or online. Given his propensity for working quickly, he has acquired a large following. By providing him with regular offerings of water, candles, and pound cake, you will establish a relationship with a powerful and speedy protector. And if you want to make a pilgrimage to New Orleans, you'll find his statue can still be found at 411 North Rampart Street, in what is now the Our Lady of Guadalupe Chapel and International Shrine of St. Jude.

St. Jude

Holy St. Jude, apostle and martyr, great in virtue and rich in miracles, near kinsman of Jesus Christ, faithful intercessor of all who invoke your special patronage in time of need. To you I have recourse from the depths of my heart and humbly beg whomever God has given such great power to come to my assistance. Help me in my present and urgent petition. In return I promise to make your name known and cause you to be invoked. St. Jude, pray for me and all those who invoke your aid. Amen.

When you're talking about miracle workers, few saints are more prominent than St. Jude. He has become famous as the "Saint of the Impossible" and "Helper in Desperate Cases." His devotees regularly publish classified advertisements thanking him for his intercessions, and it is said that no situation is hopeless once St. Jude is involved. The shrine on Rampart Street became popular in the 1930s with parishioners who had their petitions to St. Jude answered favorably. Soon regular novenas were offered at the parish in St. Jude's honor and at a shrine erected on his behalf. Later, when St. Jude Memorial Hospital in Kenner was sold to the city and became Kenner Memorial, the hospital donated its statue to the church.

To distinguish him from Judas Iscariot the Traitor, this apostle became known as Judas Thaddeus (Judas the Loving). Because he was present at Pentecost, when tongues of fire descended on the heads of the believers, his images traditionally feature a flame above his head. They also include a picture of Christ's face, which Jude is said to wear on his breast. This pays tribute to the miraculous healing of Abgar, king of Edessa. According to legend, King Abgar was cured of leprosy when St. Jude brought him a cloth impressed with an image of the face of Jesus. Thanks to this, and to Jude's eloquent preaching, Abgar and his household converted to Christianity.

St. Jude wrote one letter, the Epistle of Jude, which has become part of the New Testament. A brief note consisting of one chapter and twenty-five verses, Jude is primarily a condemnation of various false teachers who were spreading dissent and discord among the early Christians. But it has become most famous for this exhortation to the faithful, found in Jude 1:20–21.

But you, my beloved, building yourselves upon your most holy faith, praying in the Holy Ghost, keep yourselves in the love of God, waiting for the mercy of our Lord Jesus Christ, unto life everlasting.

Because he told the confused and persecuted Christians to remain steadfast and promised them an eternal reward, Jude became known as "the optimistic apostle." He also became famous as the saint who would help his devotees in the most dire circumstances, and ultimately was declared the patron saint of desperate cases.

As is often the case with early Christian saints, the history of St. Jude is cloudy at best. Legend has it that after leaving King Abgar's castle, he went out through Mesopotamia and Persia preaching the Gospel and attracting many followers. But his success—and his penchant for undoing the sorceries of the magi and their idols—incurred the wrath of the Zoroastrians who ruled the region. Ultimately he, like St. Expidité, was allegedly martyred in present-day Armenia. Alas, little evidence exists to confirm this, and no record of St. Jude is found in any contemporary reports from the region.

But while separating the truth from legend may prove challenging, there is no question that St. Jude remains popular as a powerful intercessor. The primary gift he demands in exchange for his service is recognition. Those who benefit from St. Jude's aid are expected to testify publicly of his help and his power. Many will take out advertisements thanking him for his miracles.

These classified ads are often found in newspapers in New Orleans and around the world.

Perhaps the most famous modern devotee of St. Jude is a comedian named Muzyad Yakhoob (or Amos Jacobs). Like many performers, this son of Lebanese Catholic immigrants started out small: one of his first roles was making the sound of horses' hooves on a Lone Ranger radio program by beating his chest with two toilet plungers. And as with many actors, that big break proved elusive. Jacobs's wife urged him to give up show business and find steady work. At wit's end, the aspiring comedian prayed to St. Jude, promising Jude that if he would intercede on his behalf, Jacobs would build a shrine for him.

"I never prayed for fame and fortune," Jacobs explains. "I wasn't trying to do anything but make a living. I was hoping that the radio producers would have more faith in my ability to play character roles. All I wanted was to get a house in the country, buy a station wagon, raise my kids." But St. Jude had other ideas. Jacobs—under his stage name, Danny Thomas—became a popular nightclub act and later starred in his own TV show, Make Room for Daddy. After this, he joined forces with Sheldon Leonard and Aaron Spelling to produce programs like The Andy Griffith Show and The Mod Squad. A grateful Thomas kept his end of the bargain, helping to found the shrine that would become the famous St. Jude's Children's Research Hospital in Memphis, Tennessee.

St. Roch

Oh, blessed St. Roch, patron of the sick, have pity on those who lie upon a bed of suffering. Your power was so great when you were in this world, that by the sign of the cross many were healed of their diseases. Now that you are in heaven, your power

Like many notable figures in New Orleans history, St. Roch came from the French aristocracy. His father was the governor of the city of Montpellier. But unlike the Crescent City's notorious rogues and wastrels, Roch would become famous for his lifelong piety. Born with a cross-shaped birthmark on his breast, the infant Roch abstained from nursing on days when his devout mother was fasting. In his twentieth year (approximately 1315) Roch's parents died, leaving him a sizeable legacy. Instead of squandering it on wine, women, and song, the young nobleman distributed his wealth among the poor and set out on the road as a beggar.

On his way to Rome, Roch stopped at the plague-stricken city of Aquapendente. Contemporary doctors were powerless against this disease—but Roch healed the sick simply by making the sign of the cross over them. Those he could not heal he nursed as best he could. Traveling from city to city, he ministered to the ill and unfortunate until finally, at Piacenza, he came down with the pestilence himself. Unwilling to burden others with his suffering, the ailing Roch went out to a hut in the woods and lay down to die.

But in his hour of need the holy man who had worked so many miracles was now aided by God. A dog from a nearby hovel found the ailing Roch and tended to him by bringing him bread and licking his sores. Cured of the plague, Roch set back out on his pilgrimage with his canine friend until he heard rumors of civil war in his home. Still wearing the rags of a mendicant holy man, he returned to the city where his uncle had governed since his father's death. Living on the streets he might have ruled, he preached the Gospel and worked miracles for the poorest of Montpellier's poor.

Alas, the city was on high alert for spies—and the charismatic beggar soon attracted the attention of his uncle's military forces. Arrested by the army, Roch humbly refused to reveal his identity, and none of the courtiers and politicians recognized the ragged, plague-scarred preacher who wandered about the city with his faithful hound. Roch and his dog were cast into the city's dungeons. There Roch ministered to fellow prisoners for five years until he died. When his corpse was prepared for burial, the cross-shaped birthmark was discovered, along with a document proving Roch was the former governor's son. Where once the citizens of Montpellier had locked him up as a spy, they now hailed him as a saint—especially after many who called on the now-deceased Roch reported miraculous healing.

While New Orleans was safe from bubonic plague, it suffered regular outbreaks of malaria and yellow fever. During a particularly virulent outbreak in 1867, German priest Peter Leonard Thevis called on St. Roch to protect his congregation at Holy Trinity Catholic Church. Father Thevis promised to erect a chapel in St. Roch's honor if no one in the parish should die from the fever. St. Roch answered the priest's prayer: not one member of Holy Trinity died from yellow fever in the 1867 outbreak or a later epidemic in 1878.

Today Father Thevis's chapel and its accompanying campo santo (resting place of the holy) give their name to the St. Roch neighborhood, a vibrant largely African American neighborhood that was the birthplace of noted jazz pianist Jelly Roll Morton and other musical luminaries. St. Roch's Gothic shrine is filled with testimonies to Roch's healing intercession. Cast-off crutches and braces lie next to crucifixes and cockroach carcasses; artificial eyes, feet, and other commemorative votives hang on the walls alongside thank-you notes.

If you are suffering from a disease or injury, you should definitely seek appropriate medical attention. But even doctors can use some assistance—and St. Roch has a long history of alleviating suffering. A red candle and an offering of bread and table scraps for his faithful dog can help to attract his attention. After you recover, hang a retablo (an image of a bodily part, available online or in many Mexican stores) of the area that Roch cured in his shrine—be that shrine in your home or in a church dedicated to St. Roch (also known as St. Rocco, St. Roque, and St. Rochus).

Unfortunately, St. Roch's New Orleans shrine has seen better days. After Interstate 10 was run through the neighborhood in the 1960s, property values declined and crime soared. Then in 2005 Katrina did major damage to the area's homes and businesses. Years later little has been done to repair the blight or encourage the repopulation and revitalization of this once-thriving region. We can only hope that St. Roch sees fit to work his healing magic on the place that bears his name.

THE BRINGERS OF GOOD FORTUNE

St. Joseph, Assonquer, and John the Conqueror

New Orleans has become famous for its relaxed way of life—but relaxation requires funds, and while Spanish moss may grow thick on the city's live oaks, money does not. Those who practice New Orleans Voodoo can rely on the assistance of many spirits who understand their situation. Prosperity means more than a fat bank account; it means having what you need to enjoy your life. With the aid of some of the city's favorite saints, you too may be able to keep yourself in a style that allows time for both business and pleasure.

St. Joseph

Oh, St. Joseph, you worked as a humble carpenter, earning your wages by the sweat of your brow. Assist me in obtaining my wages that I may be able to support myself and my loved ones as you supported Jesus and Mary. Oh, St. Joseph, whose protection is so great, so strong, so prompt before the throne of God, assist me by your powerful intercession, and obtain for me from your divine son all spiritual blessings, so that I may offer my thanksgiving and homage to the most loving of fathers.

After the Civil War New Orleans became a favorite destination for Italians traveling to the New World. Between 1850 and 1870 the city had more Italian immigrants than any other city in America, and the French Quarter became known as "Little Palermo" and "Little Sicily," thanks to its large Italian population. These new residents brought with them their cuisine (which is still enjoyed today in po' boys and muffaletta sandwiches) and their work ethic. They also brought with them an undying devotion to a saint who has become a New Orleans favorite—St. Joseph, the foster father of Jesus.

In Italy, as in New Orleans, one celebrates a holiday by feasting. St. Joseph is typically honored on his day (March 19) with groaning tables of food put out in his honor. This tradition has been carried over to the Crescent City. A table put out in the 1920s by Mrs. Messina, a New Orleans Italian, gives you some idea of how big these repasts can be:

I have five hundred different kinds of food. Besides the three sorts of St. Joseph's bread, I have stuffed artichokes, stuffed crabs, stuffed peppers, stuffed celery, stuffed eggs and stuffed tomatoes. I have lobsters, red snapper fish, shrimps, crayfish, spaghettis, macaronis, spinach, peanuts, layer cakes, pies, pineapples My God! I have everything!

In addition to food, these tables are also decorated with flowers, candles, electric lights, and statues of saints, with a large statue of St. Joseph occupying the place of honor. Whatever else they may contain, they always have St. Joseph's Bread (a braided egg bread that is almost identical to the challah bread served on the Sabbath in Jewish homes). They also have a large bowl of fava beans. At the end of the feast, the leftover food is given to the poor. Participants take with them a bean and a small piece of bread. The bread is kept in the house until next year; it is said that in return, St. Joseph will keep the household from going hungry. The beans are said to bring good luck. While it is traditional to leave a coin on the altar in exchange for this gift, gamblers will sometimes leave large sums of money in exchange for a lucky bean.

If you want to win St. Joseph's favor, you can make a special St. Joseph's potpourri for him. Place in a white bowl the following: Balm of Gilead buds, juniper berries, tonka beans (also known as wishing beans), fava beans, and star anise. If you can find them, add fishberries, also known as Levant berries. Fishberries were part of the original mixture catalogued by Zora Neale Hurston but can be difficult to find, as they are quite toxic and no longer widely used in conventional or alternative medicine. Basil (also known as St. Joseph's Wort) is an acceptable substitute. Put this bowl before your St. Joseph statue or image and add fresh potpourri regularly. Not only will it be a great offering, but it will fill your space with a subtle fresh scent that will draw positive energy and good fortune.

To make a powerful St. Joseph's Oil, pour this mixture into the bottom of an oil lamp and fill the lamp with high-quality olive oil. Place the lamp before your St. Joseph image, then light it and leave it burning while you say a Rosary in St. Joseph's name. When you are finished, snuff out the lamp. Repeat this for nine days (a novena). After you have said these prayers, strain out the potpourri and save the oil. You can then use the oil to anoint the doorway of your business or your workplace. You can also put a few drops on your wallet or bankbook if you are looking for a raise. As the patron saint of workers, St. Joseph will be happy to offer his assistance if you're willing to do your share and earn your money.

And while St. Joseph is typically called upon to help out in money matters, he is also a sympathetic defender of lovelorn men. New Orleanians who suspect their wives of infidelity will often come to St. Joseph for his help. They reason that since his wife had someone else's baby, he will understand their plight and come to their aid. This may seem disrespectful, but it has a long history. In medieval mystery plays, St. Joseph was often played for comic relief as a cuckolded husband. Among Eastern Christians, he was frequently presented in Nativity scenes as despondent and downhearted, unable to comprehend the great mystery of the Incarnation and filled with doubt at his wife's purity. Yet he was able to overcome those doubts, become a loving husband to Mary, and support the young Jesus as his own child. It is not surprising that he would take pity on others who find themselves in a similar situation and offer them his help.

Assonquer

Assonquer, you appreciate the finer things of this world and take joy in the pleasure of others. Grant me good fortune and bless me with your generosity. Let me live not only righteously but joyously, and let me share your benevolence with those who are in need so that we may celebrate together and sing your praises. For it is not your will that we should suffer but rather that we should rejoice and partake of the blessings that God has created for us in this life and in the next.

Many African spirits have been forgotten in the New World or never made it here. With Assonquer we find a different situation—a spirit who appears to have been forgotten on his home continent, and throughout most of the African diaspora, but who is remembered and served in New Orleans. Frequently mentioned in nineteenth-and early twentieth-century accounts of Voodoo in New Orleans and the Mississippi Valley, Assonquer (also spelled Onzoncaire) receives much less attention today. But though outsiders may have forgotten him, some still remember his power and benefit from his friendship. If you have financial problems that need solving, you may find Assonquer to be a benevolent protector and helper.

In his 1880 novel The Grandissimes, New Orleans writer George Washington Cable describes a ritual that calls on Assonquer:

The articles brought in by the servant were simply a little pound-cake and cordial, a tumbler half-filled with the sirop naturelle of the sugar-cane, and a small piece of candle of the kind made from the fragrant green wax of the candleberry myrtle. These were set upon the small table, the bit of candle standing, lighted, in the tumbler of sirup, the cake on a plate, the cordial in a wine-glass. This feeble child's play was all; except that as Palmyre closed out all daylight from the room and received the offering of silver that "paid the floor" and averted guillons (interferences of outside imps), Aurora,—alas! alas!—went down upon her knees with her gaze fixed upon the candle's flame, and silently called on Assonquer (the imp of good fortune) to cast his snare in her behalf around the mind and heart of—she knew not whom.

By and by her lips, which had moved at first, were still and she only watched the burning wax. When the flame rose clear and long it was a sign that Assonquer was engaged in the coveted endeavor. When the wick sputtered, the devotee trembled in fear of failure. Its charred end curled down and twisted away from her and her heart sank; but the tall figure of Palmyre for a moment came between, the wick was snuffed, the flame tapered up again and for a long time burned a bright, tremulous cone. Again the wick turned down, but this time toward her,—a propitious omen,—and suddenly fell through the expended wax and went out in the sirup.

Mambo Samantha Corfield, a New Orleans Voodoo priestess currently residing in Albuquerque, New Mexico, refers to Assonquer as "the Spiritual principle of propinquity." For her, Assonquer is the spirit who ensures that you are in the right place at the right time—or at the right times. Behavioral psychologists have described a propinquity effect. After extensive studies, they have determined that we are most likely to become friends, lovers, and business partners with the people with whom we interact most frequently. (Any New Orleanian, even those without advanced degrees, can tell you that success is not just about what you know but whom you know!) Assonquer can help to bring you acquaintances who are not only entertaining but also profitable.

If you want to stay on the good side of your boss—or to convince him or her that you are indispensable—Assonquer can help. Give said boss a lamb's head if you can find it (if not, a nice lamb roast, cooked rare, will suffice) and a quart of whiskey. Add a drop of your blood to some black ink, which you will then use to write your boss's name on a piece of paper nine times. Take this, and your offerings, to a nearby oak tree. After you have asked Assonquer for his assistance, leave them behind and return home. Your boss should warm up to you in a big way soon after this. Assonquer is famous for the speed with which he grants even the most difficult petitions.

In New Orleans Assonquer is frequently represented with images of St. Louis IX.   This could be a tribute to Louis' royal wealth or to Père Dagobert, the former pastor of St. Louis Cathedral in New Orleans. Père Dagobert never allowed his vows of poverty to stand in the way of his love of good food, fine clothing, and beautiful women. Although his bishop accused him of "gluttony, drunkenness and a fondness for brown women," his congregation rallied to his support, and the charges came to nothing. Some say that the Père still haunts the cathedral, wearing his beloved satin breeches and flowing lace cuffs and dipping from his bejeweled snuff box. He was certainly the sort of spiritual leader Assonquer would look favorably upon—a priest who realized that one could enjoy the pleasures of this world while preparing parishioners for the next. Green bayberry candles, cane syrup, and fine cordial liqueurs will make fine gifts for Assonquer and will help you to establish a working relationship with this well-beloved bringer of prosperity.

John the Conqueror

John the Conqueror, your kingdom was stolen from you, and you were sold as a humble slave. But you did not allow the vicissitudes of fortune to grind you down. With only your wits and your charm, you made the best of your situation and were able to get the best of those who would abuse you and take advantage of you. Look upon me with favor and grant me your silver tongue and keen mind so that I too may better myself and gain what should rightfully and justly be mine.

Blacks living under slavery, and later under the Jim Crow laws, were well accustomed to the slings and arrows wielded by the mighty against the powerless. If they were fortunate they might find work as mammies, maids, cooks, or porters, where they were expected to be properly obsequious to their white betters. Others might work as farmhands under the supervision of white overseers or as day laborers alongside whites who received higher wages for the same work. If they dared question the status quo or became too "uppity," they were liable to find themselves in jail or swinging from the nearest convenient tree.

In this milieu, "conquest" took on a very different meaning. Stories of grand heroes who emerged victorious against overwhelming odds were all well and good—but those who regularly faced overwhelming odds knew that those fights generally ended not with triumph but with tragedy. Their resistance often took the form of subverting the system and making it work for them. Overthrowing their white bosses was out of the question; getting one over on them was a more readily attainable goal.

According to African American folk tales, John the Conqueror (also known as High John or High John the Conqueror) had been a prince in Africa before he was captured by slavers and brought to America. There he was put to work on a plantation under the watchful eye of "Ole Massa." But though his circumstances were reduced, his intelligence was not. By using his wits he was able to make the most of his situation, playing practical jokes on Ole Massa and talking his way out of trouble whenever he was caught.

In one story Ole Massa came into John's cabin while he was cooking a stolen piglet. When asked what was on the fire, John told Ole Massa it was a stringy old possum. Ole Massa demanded a taste. John tried to dissuade him but Massa was insistent. Realizing he was caught, John served his Massa a big bowl of pork, telling him, "Massa, when I put this in here it was a possum, but if it came out a pig don't blame me!" Amused by John's answer, Ole Massa let him get away with his theft.

In another story, John so impressed Ole Massa with his intelligence and gift for precognition that he bet his plantation that John could guess what was hidden under a kettle. Alas, John's gift for prophecy was due largely to his talent for eavesdropping. As John walked around the kettle, he knew that Ole Massa was about to lose his bet and his plantation and that he was about to be hanged for his failure. He thought and thought about what might be hidden there, but couldn't figure it out. Finally, he threw up his hands in despair and said, "Well, you got the old coon this time." At that, Ole Massa turned the kettle over and a fat raccoon ran out. Massa won a new plantation and John won his freedom.

John's stories were told with many variants. In the Carolinas Low Country his antics combined with Cherokee folk legends and African trickster tales to become the Br'er Rabbit cycle. (In New Orleans these yarns starred Confrére Lapin.) In these stories, the smallest and most powerless of creatures managed to defeat powerful enemies like Bear, Wolf, and Fox through his superior wits. For disenfranchised, oppressed people surrounded by hostile white folks who had all the advantages over them, these myths offered hope and suggested ways by which they too could better their lot.

Today these stories make many people uncomfortable. Disney's 1946 retelling of the Br'er Rabbit legends, Song of the South, has never been released on home video in the United States because of controversy about its vision of happy black servants catering to rich whites. Lincoln Theodore Monroe Andrew Perry, who captured the "shiftless" wiliness of John the Conqueror with his Stepin Fetchit character, has been relegated to obscurity. Contemporary black Americans can express their anger openly and call public attention to the injustices that they have suffered and continue to suffer. Exploring the High John stories can give us an idea of what life was like before such open rebellion was possible—and teach us coping strategies for situations where it still is not an option.

African and Native American custom combined once again in the magical use of High John the Conqueror root (Ipomoea spp.). Named after this folk hero, this root was an integral part of a powerful mojo hand used to bring personal mastery over others and to draw luck. John was able to rely on his luck and charisma to persevere despite his troubles, and by calling on his blessings through this root, you will find that your situation improves as well. You can also call on his aid with regular offerings of pork, chicken, or other barbecued meat and with generous helpings of whiskey. If you treat John right, he will treat you right, but be sure you honor your end of the bargain. If you are stingy or forget to reward him for services rendered, he'll happily make you the butt of one of his notorious jokes.

THE ROOTS

The Dead

American culture tends to focus on the person as an individual. Our prevailing mythology honors the "self-made person" and promises us that we can become whatever we want to be no matter where we started out. The African worldview sees the person not as a discrete unit but as part of an ongoing process. You are defined not only by your achievements, but also by the ancestors who came before you and the descendants who remain after your death. You can redeem your family's sins, you can add to your family's accomplishments, or you can besmirch your family's reputation—but you cannot escape being part of your family.

While we may wish that our dead will "rest in peace," in the Kongo the deceased ancestors play a vital and continuing role in the lives of their descendents. They occupy the space between the gods and the living, and they can be called upon to offer counsel, protection, or assistance. This veneration is an important part of their religious and magical practices—and it is an integral part of New Orleans Voodoo.

The Cemeteries of New Orleans

Because most of New Orleans is below sea level, the water table is very high. A sexton who tries to dig a classic six-foot-deep grave will soon be faced with a floating coffin. When it rains the table rises even higher—and so do the deceased! A good storm will pop the caskets out of the ground and send them floating into the churchyard. Early settlers tried to avoid these premature resurrections by weighting the coffins, placing stones atop them, or even boring holes in them—all to no avail.

In 1789, during the Spanish rule, a wall vault system was placed in the new St. Louis Cemetery No. 1. Frequently used in Spain, these vaults were less prone to giving up their contents during the rainy season. After a series of 1830s epidemics were blamed on vapors from flood-disinterred corpses, the city council passed an ordinance requiring all further burials at existing cemeteries to take place in above-ground structures. In most of the United States, above- ground interment is only for those wealthy enough to afford it. The cemeteries of New Orleans are true "cities of the dead," housing the remains of the rich and the poor alike.

But as with most cities, the rich dead have more luxurious surroundings. The barrel-vaulted tombs of wealthy families, which date from the early nineteenth century, often have ornate facades and decorations. Great stone sarcophagi house those who preferred to rest in peace alone and who could afford the cost of a single tomb. Multilayered "society tombs" house those who shared common interests in life. The Orleans Battalion of Artillery Tomb of St. Louis Cemetery No. 1 contains the remains of veterans of the Battle of New Orleans, while many departed Chinese New Orleanians rest in the Soon On Tong Tomb in Cypress Grove Cemetery (120 City Park Avenue). Other society tombs house firefighters, police officers, and other working-class locals who might not have been able to afford such lavish afterlife accommodations on their own.

Offerings decorate many of these tombs. While the tomb of a famous Hoodoo queen like Marie Laveau may be covered with candles and other offerings, family members may leave toys on the grave of a deceased child, football memorabilia on the grave of a Saints fan, or bottles of beer on the grave of a departed relative who liked a drink in life. Real and artificial flowers are found in abundance in simple or elaborate vases. Clocks are found on many graves, and many graves are also decorated with shards of glass or upside-down soda bottles. This is a New World survival of the African practice of using these objects to trap or cut evil spirits.

But while these resting places are grand, they are not necessarily final. Many of the vaults are leased rather than purchased. Should no rent be forthcoming, the remains are removed. The old casket is burned and the bones deposited in a communal depository at the bottom of the structure to make way for the latest tenant. One New Orleans cemetery offered the vain but impoverished dead "three-day burials." The deceased could be interred in a fancy vault to impress his grieving friends and relatives. Three days later the remains could be cremated or disposed of in some other less expensive manner.

Even if you are not in the Big Easy, you can practice one of their most beloved customs. Each year the neighbors gather in their local cemetery for a picnic and maintenance. Tombs are whitewashed, weeds are pulled, flowers are planted or replaced, and trash is taken away. Then, after the work is completed, people sit down to share food, conversation, and memories of their dearly departed. Like the city's famous "jazz funerals," these working picnics bring together the living to celebrate the lives and accomplishments of the dead. It's a tradition that could stand to be exported—and a great way for you to make a connection with the spirits residing in your local graveyard while doing something good for your community.

Haunted New Orleans

New Orleans is a city of ghosts, with many homes and establishments boasting proudly of their spiritual stowaways. But some locations have become especially (in)famous for their paranormal activity.

Josie Arlington's Tomb

In Metairie Cemetery (which, despite the name, is located not in Metairie, a nearby suburb, but at 5100 Pontchartrain Boulevard in New Orleans) stands the tomb of infamous madam Josie Arlington. As her health failed, Arlington decided to invest her considerable earnings in a memorial. She purchased a plot in Metairie Cemetery (then the city's most prestigious graveyard) and had an enormous red granite tomb built there. Society matrons were outraged at the thought of their loved ones sharing a final resting place with Josie Arlington— especially since many of their men had already shared her bed! But there was little they could do, and when Arlington passed away in 1914, she was interred in a grand style.

Soon thereafter rumors began to spread. Reports claimed that the Arlington tomb glowed with an unearthly night during the evening, as if the flames of hell were licking at it. At the front door of Arlington's tomb stood a statue of a young girl. Some said it represented an innocent being turned away from Arlington's establishment, since Josie had always boasted proudly that no virgin had ever been despoiled in her bordello. Others said it represented the young Josie turned away from her father's house and forced into her life of vice. But the most sensational stories claimed that this statue would move at night and walk around the tombs.

Before long the Arlington mausoleum became a tourist attraction, with people visiting the Metairie Cemetery to see if the marble urns would glow with unearthly light or if Josie's statue would move for them. Her horrified family ultimately moved Arlington's remains to an anonymous grave within the cemetery. Today her former tomb is occupied by the Morales family, but it still remains a popular destination for ghost hunters and paranormal buffs. In her new, more discreet location, Josie remains in good company. Among the fellow residents of Metairie Cemetery are Confederate General P. G. T. Beauregard, jazz legends Al Hirt and Louis Prima, and Ruth Fertel, founder of the Ruth's Chris Steak House chain.

The Lalaurie House

In the early 1800s, the parties at Delphine Lalaurie's mansion were the talk of New Orleans high society. The city's finest families came to 1140 Royal Street for fine dining and sparkling conversation amid gilded furnishings. But there were whispers that the charming hostess was a cruel and sadistic woman who abused her slaves. In 1833 the streets of the Vieux Carr were buzzing with a terrible story: Mme. Lalaurie was responsible for the death of a young slave girl. The girl had supposedly run upstairs in an attempt to escape her whip-wielding mistress, but fell to her death from the balcony. Before the horrified eyes of her neighbors, Lalaurie had the girl's body buried in the courtyard. (Modern versions of the story claim Lalaurie was fined for the murder of her servant, and her slaves were sold at auction, but that her relatives purchased them and returned them to her. No corroborating historical records or newspaper accounts have been found.)

Then, on April 11, 1834, a fire ripped through the Lalaurie Mansion. When firefighters made their way into the house, they discovered several slaves chained to the wall. One old woman had been kept on her knees for so long that she was unable to stand, and a man had a gaping, worm-infested wound on his head. (The stories have become more colorful with the passage of time.

Today one hears that Lalaurie disemboweled slaves and nailed them to the floor by their intestines, stuffed their mouths with excrement and sewed their lips shut, performed impromptu sex-change operations on them, and drilled holes in their head so she could insert a stick and "stir their brains.")

Whatever happened, it led to an outraged crowd milling about the mansion's doors. Fearing for her life, Mme. Lalaurie rode off in her carriage, never to return. Some say she died in Paris, while others say she remained with relatives on the north shore of Lake Pontchartrain. And many others say that she not only returned to the city after her death, but resumed residence at her 1140 Royal Street home. Visitors have reported hearing agonized cries in the night or told tales of menacing manacled ghosts wandering the hallways along with their spectral mistress. The house is rumored to bring misfortune to those who live there. It certainly did no favors for its latest inhabitant, actor Nicolas Cage. He acquired the property in 2007, only to lose it to foreclosure less than two years later.

The Sultan's Ghost

When Jean-Baptiste La Prete found himself short on funds, he was happy to lease his winter home on 716 Dauphine Street to a turbaned gentleman who claimed to be the sultan of Turkey. The lease was signed and the sultan moved in along with his entourage. There he redecorated his new lodgings in the finest Ottoman style, with heavy carpets and draperies that protected him from the prying eyes of the rabble. (The eunuch guards who marched over the balconies and galleries with drawn scimitars served to further discourage the curious.) But the smells of opium and incense wafting from the home, as well as the rumors of wild orgies attended by the Crescent City's finest citizens, served to fuel speculation of the sultan's debaucheries.

Then, one morning, neighbors noticed rivulets of blood running out from the iron gates. Police were called. When no one answered their summons, they forced the doors and entered the home. There they found body parts scattered throughout the house; the servants, guards, harem girls, and slave boys had all literally been hacked to bits. In the garden they found a hand sticking out from the dirt; the sultan had been buried alive and suffocated before he was able to claw his way out of his shallow grave. The crime was never solved. Some claimed the culprits were pirates who wanted the sultan's treasure. Others said the sultan was really the sultan's brother, who had escaped to New Orleans after stealing gold and slaves only to find that an ocean was no shield against the Ottoman emperor's wrath.

Today the details of this story are sketchy. Some versions of the legend claim the atrocity took place in 1792, even though the La Prete House was not built until 1836. And an earlier story (compiled by historian Charles Gayarré in 1866) suggests that in 1727 a Turkish fugitive was killed in New Orleans in his cottage at the corner of Orleans and Dauphine Street—the spot on which Jean-Baptiste

La Prete later built his house! But whatever the facts behind this legend, 716 Dauphine retains a reputation as one of the most haunted houses in New Orleans. People have reported hearing the tinkle of Oriental music, the smell of incense, and bloodcurdling screams, and apparitions of a light-haired man in Turkish garb have also been spotted.

Safer Ghost Hunting

Today "ghost hunting" has become a popular hobby. People flock to graveyards, abandoned houses, crime scenes, and other sites that are purportedly "haunted" in an attempt to contact the dead.

Most deceased spirits are harmless and have little interest in the affairs of random living folks. A few are willing to play games with electrical equipment, make knocking and rapping noises, or otherwise entertain paranormal researchers. And a few are ill-disposed toward anyone who remains above the dirt. Haitians call these bad-tempered ghosts mo, from the French mort. Practitioners of Espiritismo call them "intranquil spirits"; the Japanese call them yurei; and English folk tales speak of "unsettled ghosts." All agree that they can be exceedingly dangerous.

If an intranquil spirit attaches itself to you, it can leech off your energy, leaving you weak and ill. It can cause horrible nightmares in which you find yourself reliving its death over and over. It can produce the symptoms of the disease that killed it—symptoms that no medical treatment will touch. It can try to take over your life and your body, leading to fugues or radical personality changes. If left untreated, this infestation can literally destroy you in body and soul. If you are seeking to commune with the dead, you had best be sure that you have adequate protection. A little bit of caution and common sense now can save you a whole lot of trouble down the road.

When going into places where there are active dead spirits, you should make sure you have a holy symbol on you, preferably one connected to your ancestral faith. Even if you're a lapsed Catholic or a secular Jew, a blessed crucifix or a Chai will help keep away negative spirits. Do not open yourself up to contact with any random entity who wishes to speak with you. You wouldn't lend your car keys to a stranger, so why would you let an unknown spirit into your head? A holy symbol serves the same purpose as a locked door on your vehicle. While it won't stop a truly powerful or determined spirit from getting in, it provides a layer of protection and will keep out most miscreants.

For added protection, you can carry a sprig of rue (Ruta graveolans) in your pocket. Rue strengthens your connection to elevated spirits while protecting you from intranquil or troubled ghosts. It's a very powerful and useful herb for those who wish to work with the dead. You can also use it to make a very effective floor wash: add a few drops of holy water (available in Catholic churches) and a pinch of salt, and you've got a mixture that will dissuade most unwanted ghosts from sticking around the premises. Rue is available in most botanicas and is fairly easy to grow for those who might want to add it to their indoor or outdoor garden.

In spiritual as in mundane matters, the best offense is a good defense. Don't try to send spirits "into the light" unless you know what you are doing and are prepared to have them say, "I don't want to go into the light, and you can't send me there." Exorcism is advanced work. Those who are qualified do it only with the greatest reluctance. It is grueling and hazardous labor. Don't put yourself in the line of fire without careful consideration of potential consequences. Avoid "ghost hunting" in sites where atrocities have taken place or where malevolent ghosts reputedly reside. If you don't have a good reason to speak to a killer or a murder victim, don't disturb them. They won't appreciate the intrusion, and they're likely to make their displeasure known in a painful way.

Above all else, treat communication with the dead as a sacred and a serious endeavor. To stand between here and the hereafter and speak to those on the other side is a great blessing. It is not a diversion for bored tourists engaged in spiritual slumming; neither is it a game to impress your friends. The dead carry powerful magic and can be strong allies for those who approach them with reverence and respect. They can also be fearsome enemies for those who would treat them as carnival tricks or workhouse slaves. Understand this and act accordingly and you will be fine. Ignore it at your own peril.

CANDLES

When it comes to setting a mood, there are few items as useful as the humble candle. They can turn a meal into a seductive adventure or a college bedroom into a romantic boudoir. Not surprisingly, candles can also be used to craft potent magic. Many magical folks use candles to create a "witchy" or "spiritual" atmosphere—but for practitioners in New Orleans, that's just the tip of the iceberg. Candle burning is an important part of their practice. Their candle rituals involve elaborate codes and symbols that can be used to send messages to the spirits or to effect changes in the real world.

Candles are inexpensive and versatile tools that come in a variety of shapes and sizes. Learning some of the secrets of candle magic can help you become a more competent and successful magician without spending an inordinate sum on magical items. New Orleans Voodoo practitioners have always been good at making do with available items and spellcasting on a tight budget—and if you follow their lead, you can too!

Candle Colors

Writing in 1935, Zora Neale Hurston gave the following meanings for candle colors used in New Orleans Voodoo:

White: For peace and to "uncross" and for weddings

Red: For victory

Pink: For love (some say for drawing success)

Green: To drive off (some say for success)

Blue: For success and protection (for causing death also)

Yellow: For money

Brown: For drawing money and people Lavender: To cause harm (to bring triumph also) Black: Always for evil or death

But in the 1940s another author, using the pseudonym Henri Gamache, combined old-fashioned Hoodoo with the Rosicrucian teachings of Pascal Beverly Randolph, an African American medical doctor and Spiritualist. (Randolph's teachings on sex magic inspired yet another prolific writer, Aleister Crowley.) While Gamache's real name remains a mystery to this day, his influence on New Orleans Voodoo and Southern Hoodoo is undeniable. Today most New Orleans Voodoo practitioners use the color scheme given in his 1942 Master Book of Candle-Burning.

White: Spiritual blessings, purity, healing, rest

Blue: Peace, harmony, joy, kindly intentions, healing

Green: Money spells, gambling luck, business, a good job, good crops

Yellow: Devotion, prayer, money (gold), cheerfulness, attraction

Red: Love spells, affection, passion, bodily vigour

Pink: Attraction, romance, clean living

Purple: Mastery, power, ambition, control, command Orange: Change of plans, opening the way, prophetic dreams Brown: Court case spells, neutrality

Black: Repulsion, dark thoughts, sorrow, freedom from evil Red and Black (Double Action): Remove a love-jinxing spell White and Black (Double Action): To return evil to the sender Green and Black (Double Action): Remove money-jinxing

Most botanicas stock a wide range of seven-day candles in these colors. When they have something they need to accomplish, Voodoo Queens and conjurers start out by burning one or more candles in the appropriate color or colors. A spell to sexually dominate a prospective partner, for example, might use a red (passion) and a purple (control, command) candle. A spell to bring business to your spa, by contrast, could combine white and green candles to produce a peaceful, relaxing aura that encourages your patrons to spend money.

Double-action candles in Gamache's chosen colors are widely used to remove "crossed conditions." These hexes can be set deliberately or can be the result of jealous neighbors whose evil intent alone causes harm to the target. (Italians have long recognized the power of the malocchio, evil eye, and so do practitioners of New Orleans Voodoo.) If you have had an unexplainable run of bad luck or poor health, you may be suffering from a vengeful person's evil eye. To use a double-action candle, cut off the tip and carve a new tip on the black half so it will burn first. Carve the name of your enemy on the black half and your name on the other half. This can help you send their ill wishes back to them and free you from the hex their envy and hatred has laid upon you.

After Fidel Castro's rise to power, many practitioners of Santeria made their way to America as refugees. This led to a new interest in Afro-Cuban practices, an interest that has had a great impact on New Orleans Voodoo. One popular candle is made with seven different colors of wax and calls upon the Seven African Powers—the Orishas Ellegua, Yemaya, Oshun, Obatala, Ochosi, Oya, and Ogun—to intercede on behalf of the petitioner, and can be used in times of great need. While initiates in Lukumi focus on their crowning Orisha, those who are not initiated find it most efficacious to call on several of the most well- known Orishas at once, in the hopes that one will answer their prayer.

Candle Sizes

Today the most commonly used candles are seven-day candles, also known as vigil candles. These burn inside a glass jar, making them a bit safer to use. (That being said, lit candles should never be left unattended or in a place where a child, pet, or careless roommate could knock them over.) Frequently the glass will be decorated with an appropriate saint image or figure describing the candle's intended purpose. Brown seven-day candles marked "Court Case" can be found beside green "Money Drawing," black "Breakup," and white "Uncrossing" candles. Most are made by pouring wax into the jar. Slightly more expensive "pull outs" can, as the name suggests, be pulled out of the chimney for purposes of carving, anointing, and otherwise preparing them for magical purposes. (More on this below.)

Taper candles (the kind typically used in candelabras) are used in many spells. If you can't leave a seven-day candle burning continuously, you can light a taper candle for a brief period of time while you pray and make petitions to your spirit. You can then snuff it out and repeat as necessary. Taper candles can be customized like seven-day candles with anointing oils, herbs, or markings scratched into the wax. They generally offer a short and intense burst of spiritual energy, where the seven-day candle gives a more gradual and sustained release. For situations that need a quick push, you may find a taper candle to be ideal.

Sabbath candles, sometimes called utility candles, are smaller but no less useful. These small white candles are burned by observant Jews on Friday evening to celebrate the Shabbat. They are also good to have in the house when the electricity goes out—a not-uncommon occurrence in storm-prone Louisiana. A popular Voodoo spell uses a utility candle and a jar of honey to "sweeten up" a person and make him or her more favorably disposed to you. Write the person's name on a piece of brown paper, and then write your name over that name at a 90° angle. Place the name in the honey and close the jar. Now run a match over the bottom of the utility candle until the wax is softened and stand it atop the lid. Light the candle and let it burn down. Whenever you'd like to make the person feel sweet again, repeat the purpose. In time your honey jar will come to resemble a large ball of candle-drippings, but it will grow more powerful with each use.

And if you want to petition a saint for a favor, you can use the traditional votive candle. These small candles generally come in glass holders (which can be in varying colors). They are lit before a crucifix or a statue or image of the saint. As Father Colin Donovan explains: "A Catholic who lights a votive candle, makes an offering and places an intention before the Lord. The candle symbolizes their intention, it can also stand for their presence in prayer before God, and their union, as a Christian, with Christ the light of the world. The votive element is the exchange of the offering for God's answer to their prayer."

Even if you are not Catholic, you can light these small candles in honor of your saints, your spirits, or your ancestors. Votive candles are also used in the Eastern Orthodox, Anglican, and United Methodist churches (among others), while observant Ashkenazic Jews will light a votive yahrzeit (a year's time) candle on the anniversary of a loved one's death.

Preparing Candles

Lighting a candle is only one part of a New Orleans Voodoo candle ritual. If you have a standard seven-day candle that cannot be pulled out of the chimney, you could scratch your intention into the top of the candle. If you have a pull-out, you could put it down the candle's side. If you have a specific target in mind for your working, you might carve his or her name in the wax. (If you wanted to control that person, you could carve your name atop that carving, so as to establish your dominant position over that individual.) Or you could simply write the name of the saint or spirit you are calling on, with a message like "Papa La-Bas open the door for me" or "St. Joseph please help me find a job."

Candles are also frequently anointed with oils. If you are trying to draw in positive energy—for example, if you are lighting a candle to bring a new lover or improve your business—you start anointing at the bottom of the candle and draw the oil toward the wick. While doing that, feel the energy that you are seeking pouring through the candle and up toward the wick, where it will become a bright beacon to draw your desires. If you wish to drive something away, as with a candle for uncrossing or for warding off an unpleasant neighbor, you would start at the top of the candle and pull the oil down toward the bottom. As you do, imagine the condition you want removed burning away as the wax burns, simultaneously going up into smoke and melting.

After you are done, you can roll the oiled candle in herbs or some other appropriate substance. You could roll a love candle in sugar or rose petals to make your target more sweetly disposed toward you, or in magnetic sand to draw them in your direction. If you wanted to discourage an overly enthusiastic suitor, by contrast, you might roll the candle in red pepper, black pepper, and crushed fire ants—a combination known as Hot Foot Powder, which is said to make the target irresistibly restless and unable to stay near you. A candle to High John the Conqueror might be anointed in High John Oil and then rolled in pieces of crushed High John the Conqueror root. A candle to the ancestors might be anointed with myrrh oil (since myrrh was used for embalming in ancient times) and rolled in rue to attract the benevolent dead.

While you are doing this, you can recite an appropriate prayer or petition. Psalms are used frequently in New Orleans Voodoo. With 150 to choose from, you are likely to find one that fits your specific need. If you are calling on a saint, you call on them using a prayer in their honor. (I have included some in this book, and you can find others on holy cards, at Catholic websites, or in spiritual supply stores that cater to a Catholic clientele.) If you serve spirits or deities from other pantheons, you can pray to them as you are preparing your candle. New Orleans Voodoo has always been inclusive rather than exclusive. Practitioners are open to working with any well-disposed spirit who gets them results.

You can also decorate the candle in a manner befitting your petition. Using a glue stick, you can put a saint image or holy card on the chimney. You can then decorate with glitter, glass paint, or a Sharpie or other permanent marker. With the appropriate heat-safe glue, you may even be able to add small rhinestones or crystals to the finished product. This has both an aesthetic and a spiritual purpose: the flashes of light from sparkly items serves to draw good spirits and drive away entities that are more comfortable in darkness. You can also decorate the chimney with colored ribbons. Like glitter, these are both pretty and practical: as you tie the ribbon you are "tying" spiritual energy to the candle so that it can work for your desired ends.

If you are going to burn candles, you need to be concerned about safety issues. One good technique is placing the candle in a large bowl of clean water. This will help to attract positive spirits and keep away bad ones, and it will also help prevent fires should your candle tip over. You can also fill a baking dish with sand, mixed with items befitting your cause, like herbs or charms. (Make sure the items you are using aren't flammable. If you have any doubts, put them at the edge of the dish where they aren't likely to get overheated.) You can write your petition or your target's name in the sand as well as on the candle, thereby grounding your spell in earth as well as lighting it in fire and sending it into the air.

Figural Candles

Many popular New Orleans spells use candles that are molded into a variety of shapes and images. These are particularly effective when you wish to do magic for or against a particular individual. The figural candle combines the force of the poppet or "Voodoo doll" with the magical power of fire—and practitioners often add to the mix by anointing with oils! If you want to attract someone's attention or drive someone away, you can use figural candles in a number of ways.

Penis Candles

When you want to get back at a cheating or abusive ex-boyfriend, you can use a black penis candle to "mojo his nature." Carve his name on the black penis candle and light it on a night when the moon is waning (the new moon is ideal for this). As it burns down, imagine his member falling limp and going soft, despite his best efforts to make it stand at attention again. This spell will be more effective if you have some of his personal items. Anything that contains his semen will create an intense magical bond with the candle: unwashed underwear, a stained bed sheet, or a used condom can be used to forge the link. Lacking these, you can use his signature (especially if it comes from a love letter to you or someone else!), a lock of his hair (pubic hair is especially good), a photo, or some other personal effect.

If you'd rather raise the tower than tear it down, you can use a red penis candle. Carve this with the name of your target (which can be yourself) and light it during a waxing or full moon. When the flame rises on the candle, imagine the flame rising through the penis that you are blessing so that it stands straight and tall and ready to serve. As before, you can use personal items to create a magical link between the candle and the desired recipient. You can anoint the candle with your own semen or, if you feel too self-conscious for that, some appropriate oil, like Attraction Oil, Compelling Oil, Fast Luck Oil, or whatever else best fits your plans for the weekend.

Adam and Eve Candles

These images of naked men or women can be used for all kinds of beneficial and baneful magic. If you want to bring two people together, you can set up an altar with a red Adam and a red Eve on opposite sides of the table. Scratch the target names into the candles. Burn them for a few minutes while you read the first chapter of the Song of Solomon, then put them out. Repeat this each night with another chapter until you finish with the eighth chapter; as you do, move the figures a little closer to each other until they are touching on the eighth night. (You can also do this with Adam and Adam or Eve and Eve candles. God thinks that it is good that two people should love each other and is less particular about gender than some of His followers.)

If you want to use these images for a breakup, use black Adam and Eve figurines and start the spell with the candles touching each other. Light them and read Psalm 7, then snuff the candles out. Each night move the candles a bit farther apart until they are consumed completely. Before doing this make sure you have a good reason for breaking these people apart. Psalm 7:4–5 offers a warning:

- if I have done evil to him who is at peace with me or without cause have robbed my foe—
- then let my enemy pursue and overtake me; let him trample my life to the ground and make me sleep in the dust.

Appropriate oils that could be used in these spells would be Come to Me, Follow Me Boy (or Follow Me Girl), or Marriage, if you want to make a commitment-adverse lover settle down. To accomplish a breakup you might use Crossing Oil or Break Up Oil.

Devil Candles

Devil candles may seem a bit off-putting at first. You may worry that burning a representation of Ol' Scratch will invite his Infernal Majesty into your home. But these devils aren't the bloodthirsty soul-stealers of Christian legend. These devils are not figures of evil so much as spirits of the material world. Like the Devil Tarot trump, they are connected with earthly and carnal concerns. When you have physical needs that aren't being met, you can burn a devil candle and get some assistance from those spirits who are such an intimate part of the material world with all its treasures and temptations.

Those in need of money will often rely on a green devil candle. By rubbing this fellow with Lodestone Oil or sprinkling magnetic sand on him, they hope that he will draw good fortune to them. (This is often used to get a recalcitrant debtor to pay up. By carving his or her name on the back of a green devil, conjurers hope that their deadbeat client will be tormented until such time as the bill is paid in full.) Those who are looking for some sexual fun and games (as opposed to love) may burn a red devil candle, anointed with Commanding Oil or Fast Luck Oil. And those who seek revenge may rub Crossing or Black Arts Oil on a black devil candle and ask that their enemy receive a suitably painful and memorable punishment for wrongs committed against them.

Reading Your Candle Working

The best outcome generally comes when the candle burns clean, leaving no marks on the glass chimney and little or no residue if a free-standing candle. A candle that "burns dirty," leaving a lot of soot on the glass, suggests that there are forces working against the client, and that additional work may be in order. If the flame hisses and sizzles, a smart worker will listen carefully; this may be the voice of spirits trying to communicate. And a candle that burns unusually fast may foretell quick but not lasting success in your work.

The patterns made by the melting wax from a free-standing candle can also provide information. A luck candle that melted in the shape of a four-leafed clover would be an excellent sign, as would a love candle that melted into a heart. A candle that breaks or goes out prematurely may mean the spell has failed and the worker needs to set another light. And should the candle tip over and become a fire hazard, you may need to do an uncrossing and cleansing for yourself and your client, since you are facing a powerful and malicious enemy.

OILS

Throughout the southeastern United States, rootworkers and Hoodoo practitioners swear by the efficacy of various magical oils. With colorful names like Follow Me Boy, I Will Fear No Evil, and Fiery Wall of Protection, these sweet-smelling anointing unguents are used for all sorts of magical operations. History suggests there is something to their claims; throughout the world spiritual and temporal leaders have been anointed with oil as a way of connecting them with divine power. (Indeed, Jesus Christos means, literally, "Jesus who is anointed by oil," and the Hebrew Moshiach, or Messiah, also means "anointed one.")

Oils can be used in several different ways. You can dress an appropriately colored candle with an oil designed for your intended purpose, or use it to moisten or anoint your mojo hand. You can also use it to anoint yourself and use the scent and magical properties of the oil in a combination of spellwork and aromatherapy. All these uses are regularly found in New Orleans Voodoo, and several of New Orleans' most traditional recipes have become an integral part of Hoodoo practice throughout America.

Van Van Oil

When folks in Algiers were having a run of bad luck or wanted to make sure their enemies didn't cast Hoodoo (a spell) on them, they would run down to the drugstore or their Hoodoo doctor for a bottle of Van Van Oil. This cologne (which was also available as soap, incense, bath crystals, and hair tonic) was alleged to ward off evil and offer protection. It was also believed to help charge amulets and mojo bags and was frequently added to rabbit foot charms or lodestones for luck magic.

Van Van gets its name from the Creole French pronunciation of vervaine, also known as lemon verbena. When crushed, the leaves of lemon verbena give off a distinctive sweet, complex, lemony scent with hints of licorice and mint. Lemon verbena is commonly used in herbal teas or for flavoring desserts, but it can also be used as a substitute for oregano when cooking fish and poultry. In aromatherapy lemon verbena is prized for its relaxing and sedative properties, and it is used to quell anxiety and insomnia. Folk magicians also use lemon verbena to exorcise evil, remove blocks, and eliminate negative conditions.

Lemon verbena essential oil is quite expensive and was until recently very difficult to acquire. As a substitute, perfumers used the cheaper oil of lemongrass, which smells quite similar. Since lemongrass also has very similar magical and aromatherapeutic uses, it is a very effective substitute and has become the main traditional ingredient in Hoodoo formulations of Van Van Oil. Many Hoodoo pharmacists and root doctors put flecks of iron pyrite (also known as fool's gold because of its color) in the bottle to emphasize its luck and money- drawing properties. Others add citronella and palmarosa oils to add complexity and strength to the scent. If you wish to make your own Van Van Oil, you can come up with your own formulation, using lemongrass or lemon verbena oils and going from there. (Be sure to cut them sufficiently with a neutral base like almond or olive oil, as pure essential oils can irritate the skin!)

If you need to cleanse your house, you can add Van Van Oil to a bucket of water and warm natural soap. For extra spiritual and mundane cleansing strength, add a tiny bit of ammonia. Place a few broom straws (you can get them from a used broom) in the bucket. Now wash out your domicile from back to front, sending all the dirt and spiritual bad stuff out the front door. This is known as a Chinese wash. Many rootworkers and Voodoo practitioners swear by it as an effective way to improve your luck.

It's also a very effective way to wash that so-and-so out of your life after a messy breakup. Before going into a tense or dangerous situation, you may want to put on a little Van Van Oil. Of course, you should take all necessary mundane precautions too! And if you want to put a little more money in your wallet, try anointing a $2 bill with some Van Van Oil and carrying it about with you so that it can attract some company.

Follow Me Boy Oil

As any sex worker can tell you, the world's oldest profession is also one of the world's toughest. The competition is fierce, the customers may be difficult and are frequently dangerous, and the forces of law and order are more interested in protecting decent, respectable citizens from you than vice versa. A working girl needs all the help she can get—and the working girls in New Orleans have traditionally gotten their help from liberally applied doses of Follow Me Boy Oil. This sweet-smelling fragrance didn't just attract the attention of prospective clients; it ensured that they would behave and pay well for the privilege.

There are innumerable formulas for Follow Me Boy Oil because every oil maker of the past had a particular combination of floral notes that he or she swore by. Most used rose geranium oil because true rose essential oil, also known as rose otto or attar of roses, is prohibitively expensive. Other florals that were frequently added include jasmine, tuberose, honeysuckle, gardenia, and carnation. (The latter three were invariably synthetic formulations, since the flowers in question yield no essential oil.) These were supposed to make the wearer smell appropriately sweet and feminine, like any fine perfume. To this base was added a bit of Van Van Oil. This added a lemony scent to the oil and helped to keep the heavy flowery notes from becoming too oppressive. It also took advantage of Van Van's power to drive away evil, draw luck, and strengthen the efficacy of other magical operations. Adding Van Van to a standard perfume formulation helped to amp up both the olfactory appeal and its magical power to draw male attention.

And then the final touch was added to the mix: a tiny bit of calamus root (Acorus calamus). Found in marshy areas around the world, calamus root has an unusual but pleasant fragrance that many find evocative of baby powder. Calamus was an important ingredient in the anointing oil used in the Temple of Jerusalem and by Egyptian priests. In perfumes it acts as a fixative, ensuring that the scent does not fade away too quickly, and many herbalists say it also has psychoactive and aphrodisiac qualities. But practitioners of Hoodoo and New Orleans Voodoo use it for its power to command and dominate. Calamus is a sweet, soft scent but one that subtly inspires others to do your will. Once the sweet florals attract a man's attention, the calamus, combined with the amplifying powers of the Van Van Oil, helps incline him to do the wearer's bidding.

You don't have to be a prostitute to use Follow Me Boy Oil. There are many situations where you might wish to use your feminine wiles to persuade a man. And while Follow Me Boy has most often been used by the ladies, gay men have used it to make their partners suitably pliant. Follow Me Boy may not be politically correct; all this talk of controlling men through sexual attraction may cause consternation in some feminist circles. But it is a very effective blend and one that can be used to good effect by those who wish to take advantage of its powers. It can be worn or used as an anointing oil for a mojo bag, and it can also be rubbed on a picture or other artifact of your target to gain a magical link and thereby control him in a fashion that will prove beneficial to both of you.

Red Fast Luck Oil

New Orleans is generally known as a place where things happen at a leisurely pace. But sometimes you need to get things moving, and moving fast. When folks in the Crescent City need to get their situation turned around, they use liberal doses of Red Fast Luck Oil. While some oils are meant to improve your financial situation and others are used to make you irresistible to potential lovers, Red Fast Luck Oil is an all-purpose ointment that is intended to bring you good fortune in both love and money—and quickly!

Red Fast Luck Oil begins with cinnamon oil. Cinnamon has long been used in magical and spiritual operations. Cinnamon was one of the ingredients of the holy anointing oil of the ancient Hebrews, while the Egyptians used it in mummification. Its uses as an antibiotic and a culinary supplement made it a particularly treasured spice in medieval and Renaissance Europe, and demand for cinnamon was one of the major factors behind the explorations that led to the Colonial era. In Hoodoo cinnamon is believed to heat up magical operations and is said to draw wealth and inspire lust.

Wintergreen oil is also an important component of Red Fast Luck Oil. This must be added in very small quantities, as its active ingredient (methyl salicylate) is a powerful dermal and mucous membrane irritant. But only a little bit of this sweet, sharp, balsamic-smelling oil is required. Wintergreen is said to be a powerful money-drawing oil, and it is also said to "heat up one's nature" and improve both desire and performance in the bedroom arts. (That being said, do NOT put Red Fast Luck Oil on or near your genitals. The ensuing redness will happen fast, but you won't feel at all lucky about it!)

These two hot oils are counterbalanced by a third ingredient, oil of vanilla. Vanilla acts as a cooling and mellowing agent. A drop or two of vanilla can tame the bite of an overly spicy chili or an overly acidic tomato sauce. It is also believed to be an aphrodisiac. In 1762 German physician Bezaar Zimmerman wrote that "no fewer than 342 impotent men, by drinking vanilla decoctions, had changed into astonishing lovers of at least as many women," while Dr. Alan Hirsch of the Smell and Taste Treatment and Research Foundation in Chicago found that the scent of vanilla was highly effective in increasing penile blood flow.

The red coloring is often created by synthetic dyes, but according to Hoodoo expert Catherine Yronwode, the traditional coloring agent was alkanet root. Alkanet root is also known as dyer's bugloss and is used to redden textiles, makeup, and food. (It was once used to darken the color of inferior wines and to give wine corks an aged appearance.) It was also magically employed in drawing luck and protecting money, so, as Yronwode says, "It is a better colourant for Fast Luck than any synthetic dye could ever be." But it is also a tricky dying agent: too little and you get Pink Fast Luck, while too much will turn your oil a muddy crimson brown. If you are going to make your own, you are advised to add a few flecks of alkanet root per every half ounce of oil and let it steep for a day or so until you get the desired shade of red. While it may bring you fast luck, its creation requires patience.

It also requires caution: both wintergreen and cinnamon oils can be corrosive on sensitive skin, so make sure you use enough carrier oil and test with a tiny amount to see if you find it irritating before putting on more. You would probably be better advised to use your Red Fast Luck Oil for anointing a mojo bag or using it in a floor wash to bring in a quick run of success to your business or your bedroom.

Algiers Triple Strength Oil

During the early part of the twentieth century, Algiers attracted many black Americans looking for a good time—or a good Hoodoo worker. Like the French Quarter today, the Algiers district had a thriving business catering to tourists in search of spiritual aid. Blues musicians sang of the Seven Sisters of Algiers and their magical talents, while thirsty black travelers could wet their whistle at any of Algiers' thirty-nine taverns after picking up a mojo hand or a love potion. (Indeed, many black New Orleanians took the ferry across the river when they needed spiritual work or wanted to party without worrying about color lines.)

Today Algiers has become a quieter place. The Huey P. Long Bridge ended the twenty-four-hour ferry service that connected the district with the French Quarter, while the closing of the Algiers railroad terminal in the 1970s and the oil bust in the 1980s led to unemployment and an exodus of many once- prosperous black Algerines. But Algiers still retains its reputation as a Hoodoo and Voodoo capital in many quarters, and many rootworkers still swear by the efficacy of Algiers Triple Strength Oil in their magical operations.

There are many variations in the recipes for Algiers Triple Strength Oil, but most begin with the three oils used in Red Fast Luck Oil—vanilla, wintergreen, and cinnamon. To this is added patchouli. While the smell of patchouli may evoke images of headshops and hippies in your mind, it has a long history of magical use. Its earthy fragrance is said to draw money and attract sexual passion, and to increase the magical power of other substances. Patchouli is also a fixative that extends the life of other scents and spiritual operations. It turns Red Fast Luck Oil's powerful but short-lived magical blast into a longer-lasting, mellower run of good fortune.

But Algiers Triple Strength Oil also calls on the power of numerology—more specifically, the magical number three. Three is the number of the Holy Trinity; the Three Wise Men who came bearing gifts; the three virtues of faith, hope, and charity; and the triplicity of body, mind, and spirit that is humanity. Algiers Triple Strength Oil includes three ingredients that are known for their powers in drawing money, love, and luck. Some combine magnetic lodestones with bits of High John the Conqueror root and devil's shoestring (long roots said to "trip up" the Devil while drawing money and luck to the bearer). Others include flecks of iron pyrite (fool's gold), magnetic sand, or a pinch of nutmeg (which is said to bring good fortune and is used in whole form in a powerful gambling mojo). Just about any love or money-drawing ingredients can be used in Algiers Triple Strength Oil, so long as you include three of them.

Depending on what you wish to accomplish, you can use Algiers Triple Strength Oil in a number of ways. If you are tired of sleeping alone, you can sprinkle a few drops in each corner of your bedroom and anoint your bedposts. This will work nearly as quickly as Red Fast Luck Oil but will tend to attract a longer-lasting relationship instead of a one-night stand. If you are heading out to a job interview, a dab of Algiers Triple Strength Oil behind your ears will make you magnetically attractive to prospective bosses and leave them thinking about you after you have departed. If you need to close a deal that will require extended negotiations, Algiers Triple Strength will stay with you through those all-night debate sessions. Add it to your spiritual tool kit and you'll soon find many other situations where it can give you that extra edge over your competitors.

Has No Hanna

When you first hear of Has No Hanna Lotion, you might assume it was used primarily for love spells, especially when you get a whiff of its sweet floral scent. But in the Big Easy, Has No Hanna is mainly used not by lovelorn women but by gamblers hoping to make that lucky break. When you are playing poker with an old-time New Orleans cardsharp, you might note the smell of jasmine lingering about him—and about your money after he wins it from you! Among those who know their Hoodoo, jasmine is a scent that can help you to become lucky in both cards and love.

The name Has No Hanna comes from the Bengali word for night-blooming jessamine (Cestrum nocturnum), hasnuhana. As per its name, night-blooming jessamine releases its perfume only after sundown. Its small greenish white tubular flowers are not particularly showy; gardeners typically plant more showy flowers at the base of jessamine bushes. But though their flowers are modest, they are overwhelmingly fragrant. Some find the aroma overpowering, but most find it heavenly. Although it originates in South Asia, hasnuhana has become naturalized in many tropical and subtropical climes, where it is treasured for its powerful, intoxicating scent. It is found throughout Louisiana and perfumes many a moonlit New Orleans garden.

Night-blooming jessamine is not related to the jasmine family (Jasminum spp.). It is more closely related to deadly nightshade and datura (angel's trumpet). But its scent strongly resembles that of the jasmines, as does its penchant for releasing its fragrance after dark. And while night-blooming jessamine's essential oil is almost impossible to come by and extremely expensive when you do find it, jasmine has long been cultivated for use in perfumery. As a result, Has No Hanna is scented not with Cestrum but with Jasminum flowers. Much as lemongrass has taken the place of lemon verbena in Van Van Oil, so jasmine has become the standard scent for hasnuhana's namesake lotion.

The same qualities that make jasmine so popular with romantics are also useful to professional gamblers. Jasmine promotes feelings of wellbeing and intimacy. Those who smell it are more inclined to let down their guard, thereby giving a smart player the advantage in a game of strategy. Jasmine relaxes the wearer while simultaneously clearing the mind, and some aromatherapists claim that jasmine promotes alertness and increases the memory. Those who make their living by knowing what the cards hold can use all the help they can get in these areas, and hence many New Orleans gamblers have scented their hair or rubbed their skin with Has No Hanna Lotion before an evening at the tables.

Unfortunately, many modern formulations of Has No Hanna are made without jasmine. Gardenia and rose are often combined with citrus scents like orange or tangerine. The resulting product smells lovely but is no substitute for the traditional formulation. Those wishing to make their own Has No Hanna Lotion can add some jasmine essential oil to an unscented hand cream and rub it sparingly on the hair and hands. (While you should always check for sensitivity, you will probably have no problems. Jasmine is generally considered to be good for the skin and is sometimes used for dermatitis and dry skin conditions.) You can also anoint your wallet with your homemade Has No Hanna and watch it fill with money. And if you are already in a relationship, some say that regular use of Has No Hanna will keep your lover close by you—especially if your beloved is fond of jasmine!

SPIRIT DOLLS

We all know the common cliché: the gnarled old witch doctor stabs a doll by the light of a flickering bonfire; the camera cuts to the target writhing in the throes of shrieking agony. You have probably seen "Voodoo Doll" kits, complete with pins and instructions for use on your enemy, and you may even have purchased one! Dolls are an important part of Hollywood's horror show vision of Voodoo; whether they are seen as spooky props or entertaining toys, they are certainly not something one needs to take seriously.

The Voodoo dolls beloved of New Orleans tourists are typically sticks or spoons wrapped with brightly colored yarn, then decorated with feathers and appliqués. It would be easy enough to write them off as gewgaws for the tourists, based on myths. But like many New Orleans myths, these legends have a basis in truth. Most casual observers will be satisfied with their souvenirs. Those who wish to tap in to their power will need to explore a bit deeper.

Feitiços, Fetishes, and Minkisi

An Nkisi called Kikokoo, which appears also in other records, was a man's image of black wood standing in the village of Kinga on the coast of Loango. It kept the sea calm and brought much trade and many fish to Loango. Stolen one night by two young men from a Portuguese boat, it was damaged. Therefore the young men drove nails into its head and arm in order to attach them again to the body, and, in the night, returned the statuette to the village. A story was immediately diffused by the nganga saying that Kikokoo had been to Portugal and brought back with him a boat full of merchandise. Shortly after this, a

In the Kongo, ngangas (medicine men) make a handsome living constructing magical statues (nkisi, plural minkisi) for their clients and community. The Portuguese sailors who first encountered these magical objects in the fifteenth century called them feitiços, a word they used to describe charms and amulets. Today they are commonly called fetishes. Some fetishes have the heads or stomachs hollowed out to hold special substances like earth, blood, or magical herbs. Others are decorated with horns, shells, nails, feathers, metal, twine, paint, cloth, or beads. Some of these fetish figures combine male and female attributes to hearken back to the original androgynous ancestor of all humanity. Others have two faces, so they can guard their owners from attacks in any direction. The eyes and "medicine pack" (cover for the hole that contains the secret herbs and substances that empowered the statue's spirit) are generally covered with reflective mirrors. These are intended to dazzle and frighten evil ghosts, and they can also be used for divination. By gazing into these, the ngangas are able to enter a trance state and go into the spirit world.

The nkondi (meaning "hunter," plural minkondi) fetish is used to hunt down thieves, evil sorcerers, and other threats to the community. To inspire the indwelling spirits to action, gunpowder was exploded before them and nails driven into their wooden bodies while gory invocations urged them to take bloody revenge against these enemies. An nkondi could also serve as witness to oaths. The parties would make their promises and seal the deal by driving a nail or spike into the nkondi. It was believed that should either violate the terms of their agreement, the nkondi would punish them by illness or death. An old and powerful nkondi might have so many nails and blades driven into it that it resembles a porcupine: each nail was said to have "awakened" the spirit to perform a specific task.

Someone who believed he or she had been cursed with illness might drive a nail into an nkondi to send the illness back to the spellcaster. Or the cursed individual might seek the services of an mbula, a statue covered with small gunpowder-filled tubes representing rifles. These the mbula could use to kill evil spirits afflicting an individual or a village. People might also call on a na mgonga statue, a benevolent image that was believed to bring healing and good fortune to those who propitiated it. A pregnant woman might surround a nkisi with a bilongo, offerings of clay, herbs, and other substances that were placed in cloth and then wrapped around the statue to ensure safe childbirth and a healthy infant. And while most villages have several communal minkisi, many individuals and families also had their own nkisi for protection and prosperity.

There is evidence that at least some New Orleans Voodoo Queens of the past had minkisi of their own. The statue confiscated from Marie Laveau supposedly resembled a centaur. Many minkisi statues combined human and animal elements, and Voodoo Queen Betsy Toledano claimed their society "was a religious African institution, which had been transmitted to her, through her grandmother, from the ancient Congo Queens."

While the contemporary Voodoo dolls sold in New Orleans shops are generally made in China, their design shows a Kongo influence as well. Spoons or sticks wrapped in colored cloth are regularly used as fetishes in Kongo and Bantu practices. The wrappings most commonly conceal herbs or other sacred materials that are intended to draw the spirit into the item and thereby ensoul it, something that is lacking in the tourist dolls. The feathers that decorate the top of the doll can be seen as a symbol of the lightning flash of spirit descending into the item. They can also serve the practical purpose of "giving the spirit wings": by adding artifacts from a bird, the spirit is believed to gain the power of flight.

The creators of the tourist Voodoo dolls may not have done much research into the African roots of New Orleans practices. But they (or the Chinese companies that filled their orders) reproduced Kongolese fetishes with surprising fidelity. In turn, many of the black and Creole Voodoo practitioners incorporated a common European practice into their work—the making of poppets. In time they would become so famous for these items that they would come to be identified not with European witchcraft but with African spiritual practice.

Poppets

Perhaps the most familiar application of the principle that like produces like is the attempt which has been made by many peoples in many ages to injure or destroy an enemy by injuring or destroying an image of him, in the belief that, just as the image suffers, so does the man, and that when it perishes he must die. James g. Frazer

Many magical spells are based on what James G. Frazer (author of The Golden Bough) called the Law of Similarity. If Item A resembles Item B, it can be used to influence Item B for good or for ill. In creating an image or simulacrum of your target, you build a link by which you can work magic. This concept began in the mists of prehistory. Sixteen thousand years ago Paleolithic shamans painted stags and bulls on the walls of their Lascaux cave to ensure a good hunt. During the reign of Rameses III (1187–1156 BCE), a group of priests, courtiers, and harem ladies were sentenced to death for using wax figurines to work baneful sorcery against the king and his bodyguards. Over 2,600 years later, in 1591, several people of North Berwick, a seaside town in Scotland, were executed after they were accused of making and then melting a wax image of King James VI of Scotland.

To make these images especially powerful, witches would often add to it what Frazer called the Law of Contact, or Law of Contagion. While an image could be used effectively, something directly connected with the individual would provide an especially powerful link. A lock of hair or fingernail clippings are among the items commonly used. Menstrual blood or semen are often used for sexual or love magic, and in a pinch you can even use a person's signature. (One particularly African touch common in New Orleans is using the dust from your target's footprints. It is believed that the footprint contains some of the person's essence and that an individual can be attacked through the feet with lameness, paralysis, madness, and even death.)

Poppets can be made out of many substances. You can construct a poppet using wax, clay, or even gingerbread. The poppets used in New Orleans magic are generally constructed of fabric that has been sewn into a human shape and stuffed with Spanish moss or cotton ticking along with appropriate herbs and personal effects. For example, a poppet to make an obnoxious neighbor move away might combine dust from that neighbor's footprints with dried cat manure, red pepper, and sulfur—the sort of stuff that would make you leave the area if you stepped in it! A poppet designed to kill your target may mix some of that person's hair with dirt gathered in a graveyard. A poppet to win your target's affection might be stuffed with rose petals and sugar. (Contrary to Hollywood myth, you can do much more with poppets than stick pins in them!)

Once you have constructed your poppet by whatever means you choose, you should then name it after your chosen target. The traditional Catholic way of doing this is the rite of baptism. While the full solemn rite can be performed only by an ordained priest, there is a shorter private rite that can be done by anyone. To do this you should first dress your poppet in white clothing, ideally a white gown. You will also need a white candle, preferably blessed by a priest, and some holy water (available in any Catholic church). Light the candle and say some prayers; a Rosary would be ideal. Then sprinkle your poppet with holy water and say "[target's name], I baptize you in the name of the Father, and of the Son, and of the Holy Spirit." Breathe on the poppet, and as you do, feel it being filled with the breath of life and becoming a living being with an intimate connection to your target.

Now that your poppet is properly charged, you can do for it, or to it, what you want to have happen to your target. If you wish to use your poppet in a love spell, you might surround it with candy and sweet things. Talk to it each day, telling it how much you love it and how much you want your love reciprocated. You could rub honey or cane syrup oil over its heart to make your target feel sweet toward you, and you could anoint it with Follow Me Boy Oil to encourage your target's attention. If you wish to make your supervisor more inclined to give you a raise, you might put a rope around the poppet's neck and tie it so that it is on its knees in an appropriately submissive position. You might also insert five-finger grass and masterwort (both used to gain command over a person) in the doll along with brown sugar to make your boss feel more kindly toward you. For a spell to do harm, you could use the time-honored tradition of sticking the doll with pins. You could also put the doll in a tiny coffin and bury it in the graveyard, hoping that your target dies as the doll rots away. A poppet for healing might involve regular laying on of hands and praying (or even Reiki treatments!) along with herbs intended to treat the target's condition. Your usage of poppets is limited only by your imagination.

Religious Statues and Images

Veneration of statues and images has long been controversial. In 726 Byzantine Emperor Leo III issued edicts banning the veneration of statues and icons. The ensuing outcry plunged the empire into over fifty years of religious conflict. In Europe Protestant reformers defaced many historic artworks, and today some Protestants still accuse Catholics of idolatry. And in 2001 the Taliban destroyed two enormous sixth-century Buddha statues in Bamiyan, Afghanistan, claiming they were un-Islamic graven idols. But the very existence of these arguments only proves the importance of religious and spiritual imagery.

Critics may claim that statues and lithographs lead us to worship the creation rather than the creator. Practitioners counter by saying that these images help us to move closer to that which is beyond our grasp. Images of Jesus remind us that he was simultaneously true God and true man. They make him a tangible reality to his followers, not just an arid symbol. Images help us with visualization and concentration; they help us to experience our gods on a visceral rather than a purely intellectual level. In cultures where much of the population is illiterate, images can be used to transmit ethical and spiritual teachings. The signifier helps us to reach the signified. It can serve both as a means of transmitting the artist's ideas and as a communications device allowing us to reach out toward the divine.

Statues and images were very important to the Christians of central and southern Africa. In 1491 Nzinga Nkuwu was baptized as João I, king of the Kongo. With the help of many Portuguese clergy and lay people, he and later his son, Afonso I, established a syncretic religion that combined Roman Catholicism with many traditional Kongo beliefs. As Scottish observer William Winwood Reade (a devout secular humanist and atheist with little sympathy for religion in general and Catholicism in particular) observed in 1864: "In matters of ceremonial religion the negroes are not fanatics. As long as operations were confined to baptism, to exhibiting images of the Virgin and saints, and to distributing beads, and relics, and Agnus Dei's, the people were amused and delighted by becoming Christians."

During the era of the Middle Passage, most of slaveholding America was Protestant. The slave owners and overseers would have seen veneration of Christian imagery as no less idolatrous than honor given to an nkisi or African fetish. As a result, Hoodoo in most of the United States had comparatively little usage of statues or religious images. Instead, the Protestant emphasis on studying Scripture led to a tradition of "psalms magic," which used the holy Book of Psalms and other biblical verses to work spells.

But Louisiana had a sizeable Catholic population. The high-society families who traced their roots to France and Saint-Domingue were Catholic by birth if not necessarily by devout observance. Later, immigrants from Italy and Ireland came to New Orleans. At one point the French Quarter was largely Sicilian, while the area between Magazine Street and the river became known as the Irish Channel. These believers had no qualms about showing their devotion through artworks. Early New Orleans Voodoo temples were traditionally filled with statues of saints, virgins, and angels alongside African and other images. (One of Doctor John's most prized possessions was an elaborately carved elephant tusk, while Marie Laveau reportedly kept statues of a lion and tiger on her altar for "bad work" or combat magic.)

The saints sometimes stood in for African spirits, as in the case of St. Michael the Archangel becoming Daniel Blanc or St. Anthony of Padua becoming Yon Sue. But they were also honored in their own right as powerful protectors and wonder-workers. This is not surprising, given the Kongo emphasis on honored ancestors and spirits as intercessors between God and man. But whether they were seen as African spirits or saints, the treatment accorded their images was much the same. They were feted with flowers, food, drink, and candles by devotees who spoke to them as if they were alive—because those devotees believed they were!

From a magical standpoint, this makes perfect sense. Many psychics have noted that a child's well-beloved toy can take on a life of its own. (Bill Watterson was on to something when he chronicled the adventures of Calvin and his stuffed tiger Hobbes.) By giving energy to an image, you create a thoughtform that grows stronger with repeated feedings of attention and offerings. This process becomes far stronger when this image has already been fed by millions of worshippers before you. The many images of the Virgin, for example, have been fed for centuries and have been credited with numerous miracles. By setting up a saint image in your home or temple, you simultaneously tap in to and further empower a well-established egregore—a thoughtform that has been fed by generations of spiritual workers and worshippers.

If you don't want to put up a holy statue in your house, you can use a doll. These are commonly used by Spiritualists as receptacles for spiritual energy and homes for their noncorporeal friends. You can write the name of the spirit or saint on the doll's body in appropriately colored ink. Black might be used for a death deity, red for a war spirit, green for a fertility goddess, blue for an ocean or water god. You could also use the colors most commonly associated with that spirit. (Silver or gold ink is almost always acceptable.) Dress the doll in appropriate clothing, and place it in a position of honor. Feed it regularly with offerings and conversation, and listen for any words of wisdom it may wish to share with you.

This technique can be applied to spirits besides those commonly served in New Orleans Voodoo. The Voodoo Queens were always open to working with any entity that was well disposed toward them and that could produce results. If you have already established contact with a spirit guide, you can give it a home in an appropriate image. This can help you to develop a more concrete and personal relationship and improve your communications. By providing offerings to your spirits, you strengthen them and ensure greater success in your petitions. Reciprocity applies in the spirit world as well as in this one. Those who give generous gifts are far more likely to receive abundant rewards.

FORETELLING THE FUTURE

Folks in New Orleans may live for today, but that doesn't mean they aren't concerned about tomorrow. The future is a scary place, especially if you're living from paycheck to paycheck or just wishing you had a paycheck to live from. Inside information may make the difference between avoiding a crisis and getting crushed by it. As a result, many New Orleanians call on the services of a diviner to get them through tough times and provide them with leads for a more prosperous future.

Divination has long played an important role in African cultures. The Yoruba peoples have divination by cowries, coconut pieces, and the Table of Ifa, a complex system involving palm kernel nuts thrown on a consecrated surface. The Bantu peoples use knucklebones or small tablets to foretell the future. The Mande use sand divination, while the Xhosa diviners of southern Africa speak to the ancestors and spirits in shamanic trance. While many of these specific techniques were lost during the Middle Passage, the descendants of these prophets incorporated new methodologies into their practice.

Crystal Balls

For centuries the Romani people have been persecuted, enslaved, and vilified by dominant cultures that considered them born criminals and thieves. But they have also been romanticized as free-spirited, hot-blooded, happy wanderers who possess great spiritual wisdom along with an innate talent for dance and music. It is not surprising that many black Americans identified with their suffering, or that many African American fortunetellers incorporated and still incorporate "Gypsy" imagery into their practices. Many readers and root doctors claimed a touch of Rom ancestry or affected Rom styles of clothing—flowing dresses, brightly colored turbans, and abundant gold jewelry. They also incorporated one of the favorite tools of the "Gypsy fortuneteller"—the crystal ball.

In doing so, they were appropriating a cultural item that the Roma had themselves appropriated only a few years earlier. Wealthy medieval and Renaissance magicians frequently counted crystal gazing spheres among their tools. The notorious Elizabethan magician, mathematician, and spy John Dee used a crystal "shewstone," or gazing stone, to compile his influential Enochian manuscripts. But with the rise of the Industrial Age and the Victorian interest in Spiritualism, more reasonably priced crystal balls became a popular tool for inducing mediumistic trance. Large glass or crystal balls became a popular part of the stage mentalist's paraphernalia and soon became identified with diviners of every stripe, including Roma readers.

The crystal ball is merely a tool used for scrying, or seeing visions in a medium. Mirrors were often used for this purpose (hence the magic mirror used by Snow White's evil stepmother in the fairy tale and the mirrors placed on Kongo nkisi statues). So were bowls of water darkened with ink, sometimes called "witches' mirrors." By gazing intently into a translucent surface, scryers calm their minds and enter a hypnagogic state. The limited visual input of a uniform field of color causes the brain to produce images and patterns amid the blankness—a phenomenon that paranormal researchers call the Ganzfield Effect, a German term meaning "complete field."

To use a crystal ball, sit quietly in a darkened room; candlelight is good for this, as the flickering light will also serve to encourage a trance state. Make sure you are comfortable and relaxed but not so relaxed that you fall asleep. Now gaze into the center of the crystal. Don't strain yourself; watch intently but not intensely. In time you will see clouding within the crystal. Watch the clouds and let them drift. In time they will form images, then sequences of images. Don't try to interpret them or force them to appear. They will come when they come. You may want to use a tape recorder to describe what you see, or you may want to write down brief notes. If the latter, don't get too detailed as that may break you out of the trance state.

The ability to scry requires a certain innate talent. It requires practice to separate true visions from wish fulfillment and even more practice to learn how to interpret those images correctly. Some pick up crystal gazing immediately, while others require more practice, and a few are never able to master the art. (John Dee required the services of a scryer, Edward Kelley, since he had no gift for seeing visions.) If you've spent hours staring into a crystal ball with nothing to show for it but headaches, don't despair. You may be able to benefit from another technique popularized by Romani fortunetellers—tasseomancy, or foretelling the future in tea leaves.

Tea Leaf Reading

Although in America tasseomancy is most commonly associated with the Roma, it was also extremely popular among English, Scottish, and Irish psychics and fortunetellers. All that is required is a cup, some hot water, and a bit of loose-leaf tea prepared in a pot and poured into a white cup so that some tea leaves remain in the brew.

Sip the tea slowly, savoring the flavor. (You should be sure to use a good tea, and be advised that once you've enjoyed properly made tea, you may never return to tea bags again!) When you are almost finished, hold the cup in your left hand and swirl the leaves three times round in a clockwise direction. Then turn the cup upside down on the saucer and let the remaining liquid drain away.

Turn the handle of the cup toward the querent (the person seeking information). If you are reading for yourself, turn the handle so it faces you, then lift the cup and examine the inside. The leaves, and the white porcelain spaces that show between the leaves, are then scanned like a Rorschach blot for symbols and images. You may see houses, human figures, animal shapes, letters, or other forms in the cup. These can then be interpreted through intuition or in accordance with one of the many guidebooks on the subject. (Cicely Kent's Telling Fortunes by Tea Leaves and Tea-Cup Reading and FortuneTelling by Tea Leaves by "A Highland Seer" are both in the public domain and available on the Internet.)

If you don't like tea, you can also read the grounds in a cup of Turkish coffee. The methodology is similar. Oenophiles can read the dregs in the bottom of a glass of red wine, while beer lovers can read the patterns in the foam that remains after they have consumed their drink. (This may prove particularly useful when you are doing a late night bar crawl through the Quarter and want to chat up that attractive person across the room. If you have a hard time focusing on the suds, consider it an omen that you should go home.) And if you want to take your tasseomancy to the next level, you can purchase specially designed cups that feature zodiac signs or images of playing cards on the inside. These will allow you to combine cartomancy or astrology with your leaf reading.

Cartomancy

There is controversy as to whether playing cards originated in China, India, or the Islamic world. But what we do know is that by 1377 a Paris ordinance forbade card games on workdays and that on May 14, 1379, Duke Wenceslas of Luxemburg and Duchess Joanna of Brabant spent four peters, two florins (the cost of eight sheep) to purchase "a pack of cards." The Italians enjoyed tarocchi, trick-taking games that resemble a more complex version of the modern Spades. The various trumps represented the social classes of medieval and Renaissance Italy, along with religious concepts and figures, like the Last Judgment and the Pope. The suit cards comprised swords, coins, cups, and wands from one to ten, along with court cards representing royalty.

While there is ample evidence of gambling and gaming with cards from the late fourteenth century onward, there is less of a record of cards being used for divination. A 1540 book by Francesco Marcolino de Forlì entitled Le sorti intitolate giardino d'i pensieri (The Oracle called Garden of Thoughts) detailed a method of drawing nine cards from the coins suit and checking them against oracular verses printed elsewhere in the book. Later evidence suggests that several Venetian women were accused of witchcraft for using trump cards in magical spells.

Then, in 1781, Antoine Court du Gébelin claimed that the Tarot originated in ancient Egypt. The trumps, according to him, represented the survival in pictorial code of their ancient religion, preserved by the pharaoh's priests. He believed Tarot cards were brought to Europe by the Gypsies (who were at that time believed to originate from Egypt, hence the name). There they were treated as mere game pieces until the time was ripe for their secrets to be revealed—and du Gébelin, of course, was the man to reveal them. Later research would indicate that the Rom originated in India rather than Egypt and that Egyptian religion bore little resemblance to the "secret wisdom" du Gébelin had "discovered" in the Tarot. But the legend survived despite the facts, and the use of cards for divination became popular with the spiritually advanced and with those seeking to present themselves as such.

Although Tarot cards were associated with the Rom and ancient wisdom, most New Orleans readers used regular playing cards for their work. The Jeu Lenormand style of reading, which removed cards two to five from the deck and assigned specific meanings to each of the remaining thirty-six, was common among Francophone natives, while Anglophone readers might use the same style and call it "Gypsy Witch." Still others might use the cards as props for a "cold reading" or as an aid to their intuition. Today many readers still swear by the Lenormand method, claiming it produces less esoteric and more down-to-earth readings than the Tarot. Those wishing to learn the method may wish to pick up a pack of "Madame Lenormand's Mystic Cards of Fortune" or the "Gypsy Witch Fortune Telling Playing Cards" and study the accompanying brochures.

In 1992 Louis Martinié and Sallie Ann Glassman created a Tarot deck that paid homage to the city of New Orleans and the spiritual practices found there. The New Orleans Voodoo Tarot reimagined the four suits as the Four Cults of Voodoo—Santeria, Petwo, Congo, and Rada. The interpretations of the various cards were influenced by Thelema, Kabbalah, and Western ceremonial magic as well as by African American, Haitian, and Cuban mythology. The lwa of Haiti mingled with the Orishas of Cuba and New Orleans historical figures like Doctor John and Marie Laveau. Glassman's artwork is powerful and evocative, and the accompanying text from Martinié includes suggested offerings and meditations.

Like the Thoth Tarot (a deck influenced strongly by Aleister Crowley's philosophy), the New Orleans Voodoo Tarot requires serious study and concentration. Those accustomed to the standard Rider-Waite deck may find it confusing or off-putting. But those who are willing to put in the effort of meditating upon the various images and studying the systems that influenced Martinié and Glassman (and reading Glassman's later text on the images, Vodou Visions) will find their efforts are richly rewarded. While their deck owes more to the contemporary New Orleans Voodoo espoused by Charles Massicot Gandolfo than to historical practices, it is still a powerful and useful tool for divination, meditation, and spiritual growth.

Dream Interpretation and Policy Books

In Genesis 41:1–41, Joseph rises to prominence in Egypt through his skill at interpreting Pharaoh's dreams. Ailing Greeks would spend the night in the temple of Aesculapius at Epidaurus, hoping that they would dream a cure for their illness. Carl Jung believed dreams provided direct communication with the subconscious mind and the world soul, which he called the "collective unconscious." Dreamers in New Orleans generally aimed for a less lofty goal. They believed that by correctly reading their dreams, they might find their lucky numbers.

Louisiana has a long if not always honorable tradition of gambling. In 1868 the Louisiana Lottery Company received a twenty-five-year charter as the state's sole legal lottery provider. (Numerous attempts to challenge this monopoly were defeated with the help of another time-honored Louisiana tradition, bribing legislators.) By 1878 it was the only legal lottery in the country; as a result, over 90 percent of its revenue was coming from outside the state. In 1895 an act of Congress prohibited the interstate sale of lottery tickets, and the Louisiana Lottery was disbanded. An investigation of its business revealed corruption on a scale that shocked even hardened Louisianans. By 1900 thirty-five states had constitutional prohibitions against the operation of lotteries.

But this did not stop entrepreneurs from running "policy" rackets. Bettors could buy a policy of four numbers from a numbers runner or at a policy shop (which was often a tavern or other public establishment). Those who picked the winning number received a payout, which was typically 600 to 1. Since the odds of winning were 1,000 to 1, this meant that bookies were able to make a tidy sum even after paying overhead to runners, shopkeepers, and police officers. During the 1880s, policy booths ran openly in the streets of New Orleans, taking bets ranging from a few pennies to $40. After the turn of the century, they went underground but remained popular with black and white clients alike.

To gain an advantage in the game, players turned to their dreams. But though they might not have been acquainted with Freud or Jung, they knew that the language of dreams was often subtle and symbolic. This led to a thriving business in policy dream books, which translated dream images into lucky numbers. The grandmother of these, Aunt Sally's Policy Players Dream Book, was first published in 1889 (and remains in print today!) but competitors soon produced their own dream guides. A few of the more popular ones include King Tut Dream Book, Policy Pete's Dream Book, and Stella's Success from Dreams (not to be confused with Stella's Lucky Seven Star Dream Book).

It was never entirely clear how these books distilled numbers down from imagery. Policy Pete suggested that a dream of coffee meant you should pick 098, while if you dreamt of a coffee shop you would go with 633. (Presumably if you were drinking coffee in the shop, you would make two bets to be on the safe side.) But Mother Shipton's Gipsy Fortune Teller and Dream Book warned that dreams of coffee portended misfortune or meant that you should bet on 11, 12, and 39. Rajah Rabo's Dream Book (first published in 1932) advised that if you dreamed of a colored dope fiend, you should bet 037. A dream of a white dope fiend would mean betting 778. But though their numerological reasoning might be opaque, bettors swore by their favorite policy books and scorned all others as pale imitations.

Many of the books also included advice based on the bettor's sun sign, numerological analyses of names and addresses, and other factors. Several included Napoleon's Book of Fate and Oraculum, a divinatory system that had reportedly been used by the Little Emperor after he discovered it during his campaign in Egypt. (The oracle uses scratches on paper to form random figures and is actually a simplified form of classical Arabic geomancy.) The Old Gipsy's Dream Book and Fortune Teller taught basic palmistry and a system of divination using dice as well as offering dream interpretation.

You may not be a gambler, but you can still benefit from writing down your dreams and studying them. Many cultures have believed that it is possible to speak with gods, spirits, and ancestors while asleep. And even the most die-hard secular atheist will have difficulty denying the creative potential of dreams. Paul McCartney awoke from a dream with a melody in his head; he transcribed it on the piano, and it became the classic song "Yesterday." Mary Shelley turned a nightmare into a classic novel, Frankenstein, as did Robert Louis Stevenson (The Strange Case of Dr. Jekyll and Mr. Hyde) and Stephen King (Misery). German scientist Friedrich Kekulé dreamed of atoms dancing in a circle and awoke to an understanding of the mystery of the benzene ring. American inventor Elias Howe dreamed of natives carrying spears with holes in the point and was inspired to create the sewing machine needle.

Working with dreams is almost as easy as falling asleep. Indeed, getting enough sleep is one of the most important things you can do to have both better dreams and better health. Researchers have found that people who get between seven and nine hours a night have lower rates of cancer, depression, and heart disease as well as improved memory and cognitive function. Keep a pen and paper by your bedside and write down your dreams immediately upon awakening. In time you will see recurring themes and possibly even answers to problems that have long perplexed you in waking life.

9 781803 621319